MICHEL CORRETTE
and
FLUTE-PLAYING IN THE EIGHTEENTH CENTURY

by

Carol Reglin Farrar

Musical Theorists in Translation
Volume IX

MICHEL CORRETTE

AND FLUTE-PLAYING IN THE EIGHTEENTH CENTURY

by

CAROL REGLIN FARRAR

INSTITUTE OF MEDIÆVAL MUSIC, Ltd.
1653 West 8th Street BROOKLYN, New York USA 11223

Internationale Standard Buchnumerierung 912024–29–1

Imprimé en Allemagne par Helmut Gruber, Minden (Westf.)

To

Edwin

ACKNOWLEDGEMENTS

Many friends have contributed to the completion of this book, and I sincerely thank all of them, even if only several can be mentioned here. To Mr. Mark S. Thomas is extended appreciation for helpful suggestions relating to my presentation of facts about the flute, and I am indebted to Dr. Gordon H. Smith for patiently reviewing the translation with me. A special acknowledgement is due Dr. George C. Schuetze, Jr. for advice and guidance, examination of drafts, and for his interest and encouragement in having this work published. I am also grateful to the staff of the Music Division at the Library of Congress for coutesies shown me as I worked with materials from the Dayton C. Miller Collection.

TABLE OF CONTENTS

Introduction

Michel Corrette

METHOD FOR EASILY LEARNING TO PLAY ON THE TRANSVERSE FLUTE

Part 1

Part 2

Chapter I

INTRODUCTION

The early transverse flute became a most popular instrument during the eighteenth century. As many anonymous tutors dating from this period suggest, playing the instrument was a fashion of the day. Its popularity is also evidenced in the vast amount of literature and music written for it.* Its importance over that of the recorder is summed up by François A. P. de Garsault, ** who, describing the various functions of the instruments in his encyclopedia, says that the transverse flute is used for accompaniment, while the recorder is used merely for amusement.

The following pages are devoted to a study of the one-keyed transverse flute and a comparison of it with the modern flute. Particular attention is given to the various methods of articulation as advocated by early writers. A brief section is also concerned with certain effects produced on the eighteenth-century flute which seem to foreshadow the accepted practice of today in using the vibrato. Such a study has been rewarding and worthy of investigation, and it has revealed enlightening facts, which hopefully, are recorded in these pages.

The flute and flute literature contained in the Dayton C. Miller collection now in the Library of Congress afford a fine opportunity for research about the flute. In personally examining the early flute, one may readily understand the statement made by Sir John Hawkins, *** writing in 1776, who says that the "... transverse flute still retains some degree of estimation among gentlemen, whose ears are not nice enough to inform them that it is never in tune."

Information contained in many old treatises is valuable for both historical and performance purposes. An English translation (with commentary) of one of these comprises the actual subject of this study: Michel Corrette's *Methode pour apprendre aisément à jouer de la flute traversiere*.

---

* See Dayton C. Miller, *Catalogue of Books and Literary Material Relating to the Flute* (Cleveland: The Judson Co., 1935).

** François A. P. Garsault, *Notionnaire ou Mémorial raisonné de ce qu'il y a d'utilité et d'intéressant dans les connoissances acquises depuis la creation du monde jusqu'à présent* (Paris: Chez Guillaume Desprez, 1761), p. 633.

*** Sir John Hawkins, *A General History of the Science and Practice of Music*, 5 vols. (London: Payne and Son, 1776) New edition, 3 vols. (London: Novello & Co., 1853). Reprinted, 2 vols. (New York: Dover, 1963), II, p. 739.

Chapter II

THE GERMAN FLUTE

Although illustrated earlier, the transverse flute is finally discussed in 1511 by Sebastian Virdung* and is mentioned by Michael Prætorius (1619)** and Francis Bacon (1627).*** In 1636, Marin Mersenne**** describes the transverse flute as being a keyless, cylindrical instrument used in military bands. The Principes de la Flûte traversière by Hotteterre-Le-Romain in 1707***** is the first treatise written for the transverse flute which establishes the fact of its acceptance and use in the early eighteenth century.

The early transverse flute without even one key could not be played in all keys of music. We learn from Johann Joachim Quantz (1752)****** that this flute had been fashioned in Germany (hence the term "German flute") and was lower in pitch than the later, one-keyed flute. He credits the addition of the D# key to the French, an innovation probably introduced within that century, Philibert******* being the first good player. In the late seventeenth century, the body of the flute was changed from cylindrical to conical in an effort to improve both tone and intonation. Early models may well have been constructed by Henri Hotteterre, musician and instrument maker in Paris. The one-keyed, conical flute was used throughout most of the eighteenth century.

---

* Sebastian Virdung, *Musica getutscht und ausgezogen durch Sebastian Virdung* (Basel: 1511). Facsimile ed. (Berlin: Rob. Eitner, 1882), p. 14.

** Michael Prætorius, *Syntagmatis musici tomus secundus Organographia* (Wolfenbüttel: Elias Holwein, 1619), p. 24.

*** Francis Bacon, *Sylva Sylvarum: or A Natural History* (London: 1627), II, Century III, 221, p. 52.

**** Marin Mersenne, *Harmonie universelle: The Books on Instruments* (Paris: 1636). Trans. by Robert Chapman. ('s-Gravenhage: Martinus Nijhoff, 1957), pp. 310-315.

***** Hotteterre-Le-Romain, *Principes de la flute traversiere, ou flute d'Allemagne. De la flute a bec ou flute douce, et du haut-bois* (Paris: Christophe Ballard, 1707).

****** Johann Joachim Quantz, *Versuch einer Anweisung die Flöte traversiere zu spielen* (Berlin: Johann Friedrich Voss, 1752), trans. Edward R. Reilly (New York: The Free Press, 1966), p. 30. References are made to the English translation.

******* *Ibidem*, p. 30. A. G. Badger, *An Illustrated History of the Flute* (New York: The Author, 1853), p. 8, definitely credits Philibert with having added the D♯ key as does Richard Carte, *Sketch of the successive improvements made in The Flute* (London: Rudall, Rose, Carte & Co., 1855), p. 8. In his *History of the Flute* (New York: The Author, 1921), p. 14, David Ehrlich says that the D♯ key was added presumably by a French flute maker about 1670.

The addition of the D# key did much for popularizing the German flute as it extended the range upward and made it possible to play chromatically in any key. The flûte-à-bec (recorder) which was still in use, could not boast of such assets. The one-keyed flute, although faulty, also had better tone quality and intonation.

The flutes were made mostly of wood, boxwood and ebony being the most popular.* Ivory was also used as well as other materials.** Attention was given to trim and decoration, and many flutes were inset with jewels or ornately carved. Ivory was considered a fine decoration on an ebony flute. The single key was of silver or brass.***

Being of wood, the flutes were greatly affected by temperature changes and moisture, and they cracked easily. As a pitch standard had not yet been established between localities, the player had to equip himself with extra middle joints for lengthening or shortening the instrument to lower or raise the pitch respectively.**** At first there were two pieces which differed from each other by about a semitone and also made carrying the instrument in the pocket easier.***** Quantz ****** reports later that six middle pieces now formed an interval slightly larger that a major semitone, and that two more could be added if necessary. However, this method could not have been satisfactory, for the inserting of a piece of one length, while correcting certain notes, only serves to make others out of tune. An invention of Quantz ******* was the addition of a tenon to the head joint to lengthen it for pitch adjustments. This was to remedy the need for extra middle pieces.

The range of the German flute extends from d' to a''', including all chromatic tones.******** There were experimental fingerings to expand

---

* Quantz, *opere citato*, p. 34-35.

** Ehrlich, *opere citato*, p. 28, lists leather, porcelain, horns, bones, etc. as materials for flutes.

*** See p. 24.

**** William and Sydney Powell, *The Flautist's Guide* (Birmingham, England: 1933), p. 91, A = 415-429 was Classical Pitch. In 1878, the French government set it at 435. See also p. 25.

***** Confer p. 24.

****** Quantz, *opere citato*, p. 32.

******* *Ibidem*, p. 32. This movable plug is attributed to Buffardin by Antoine Mahaut, *Nieuwe manier om binnen korten tyd op de dwarsfluit te leeren speelen* (Amsterdam: J. J. Hummel, 1759), p. 2.

******** See pp. 32-33.

the range of the instrument just as we do today, for d'''', etc. Michel Corrette* suggests playing low c# (c#') by fingering it the same as for low d (all holes covered). The player changes the pitch by rolling the flute in for c#' and out for d'. Hotteterre (circa 1765)** lists the fingering for c#' but goes on to say that c#' and d' are not effective notes on the flute. He also shows an upward extension of the range by giving fingerings for high a''', b''', c''', c#''', and d'''.*** These notes are produced by blowing very hard, but they are greatly out of tune and are not found in music of the times.

Experiments in constructing flutes were also effected during the eighteenth century. According to Quantz,**** the addition of keys for low c' and c#' was advocated but apparently failed as it would harm the intonation of the instrument. The addition of keys was also condemned by others,***** including W. N. James****** who said, "these notes are excrescences and are grafted most artificially on the tube of the natural flute." The C and C# keys were re-introduced by Johann Tromlitz in 1786.*******

Quantz added another D# or Eb key while in Paris in 1726 to account for a small descrepancy between D# and Eb.******** Apparently his invention was not generally known for only years later is it discussed by other writers. Georg Sorge********* critically analysed Quantz's two keys and rendered them as being unjustified. Tromlitz,********** on the other hand, found them useful.

---

* See p. 62.

** Hotteterre-Le-Romain, *Methode pour apprendre a jouer en tres peu tems de la Flute traversiere, de la Flute a bec et du Haut bois* (Paris: Chez Mr. Bailleux Md. de Musique, circa 1765), p. 8.

*** See also John Gunn, *The Art of Playing the German Flute on New Principles* (London: 1793), p. 1; François Devienne, *Nouvelle Methode pour la flute* (Hamburg: Jean August, 1795), p. 17; and Antonio Lorenzoni, *Saggio per ben sonare il flauto-traversa* (Vicenza: Francesca Modena, 1779), Table I.

**** Quantz, *opere citato*, p. 34.

***** Just. J. H. Ribock, *Bemerkungen über die Flöte....* (Stendal: Dan Christ, 1782), p. 13; and Johann Tromlitz, *Ausführlicher und gründlicher Unterricht die Flöte zu spielen* (Leipzig: Adam Friedrich Böhme, 1791), pp. 42-44.

****** W. N. James, "Essay on Fingering," in *The Flutonicon*, XIII (February, 1846), pp. 3-4.

******* Ehrlich, *opere citato*, p. 14. Cornelius Ward, *The Flute Explained...* (London: The Author, 1844), p. 6, gives credit to Floria for having revived the C and C♯ keys.

******** Christopher Welch, *History of the Boehm Flute* (London: Rudall, Carte & Co., 1883). Facsimile of the reprint of 1892 ed. (New York: McGinnis & Marx, 1961), pp. iii, 9. Quantz did not advocate tempered tuning and insisted that the second key be added to make four notes "true": d♯', a♯', d♯'', and g♯''. See Quantz, *opere citato*, pp. 46-47 for further explanation.

********* Georg Sorge, "Anmerkungen über Kerrn Quantzens", in the *Königlichen Historisch-Kritischen Beyträgen zur Aufnahme der Musik* (Berlin: 1758) IV, p. 1-17.

********** Tromlitz, *loco citato*.

In the eighteenth century, there were other experimental flutes constructed with various numbers of keys, four, six, and eight being the most noteworthy. However, these additions were met with opposition. Lew Granom, * writing about the year 1770, states that the only reason for having more keys was to draw public attention to the instrument. In language too colorful to deprive the reader, he concludes that if people think that by adding keys the flute will be more in tune, they are mistaken:

> ... blowing in tune does not depend so much upon the Flute as upon the Player; for a Performer, who has a good Ear, will play in Tune, even on a very indifferent Instrument, so soon as he has found its defects; which is not hard to conceive, since every Note on the flute may be blown either Sharper or Flatter at the will of the Performer.

He summarizes by saying that those who cannot play in tune without additional keys will not be able to play in tune with them.

Chapter III

A COMPARISON OF THE GERMAN FLUTE AND THE FLUTE OF TODAY

The German flute has many imperfections. To begin with, the embouchure hole is small and either round or oval ** as compared with the elongated square or round hole on the modern flute. On the former, the lips rest directly on the body. There is no lip plate to which we are accustomed on the flute today.

The principle of blowing is essentially the same, that is, blowing obliquely or across the hole to split the air column on the edge opposite the lips. A statement by N. Swaine *** that the breath must pass almost "perpendicularly down from the mouth to the chin" is radical indeed. On the contrary, it seems necessary to turn the German flute outward as well as blow across the hole more than on the modern one.

The tone holes are often unequally distributed on the German flute which makes for poor intonation. Because of the awkward spacing of these holes, the fingers must stretch to cover them. Of course, on our modern scientifically-designed instrument, the tone holes are precisely bored and keys built to facilitate fingering.

---

* Lew Granom, *Plain and Easy Instructions for Playing on the German-Flute* (London: T. Bennett, 1766), p. 10.

** According to Ehrlich, *opere citato*, p. 32, the oval embouchure hole was used from 1724 on.

*** N. Swaine, *The Young Musician, or the Science of Music* (Stourport: G. Nicholson, 1818), p. 42.

There is a very real problem of intonation on the German flute. The low notes are weak and have a dull sound. An even volume is unobtainable as some of the notes are muffled, i.e., G♯ and F, while others are reasonably clear. It is necessary to adjust the pitch of each note with the lips and by turning the flute in or out. Octaves are poor and require a keen ear to set them. This is not to say that today a player can simply blow his flute and have all the notes be in tune, but at least the modern flute is so constructed that a person finds only a minimum of adjustment necessary. The notes in the third octave of the German flute are of inferior quality and are very sharp. Similarly, players today must be cautious about blowing the high notes sharp.

Because of its structure of wood, the older instrument has little resonating power; therefore, dynamic changes are difficult to execute. One can hardly produce a good *forte* sound with which to contrast a soft echo. The dynamic range seems rather to be limited between *mezzo-forte* and *mezzo-piano*. The metalic flute of today is capable of a wide variety of dynamic differences. It is interesting to note how well the early flute was praised for having many powers of expression and for closely imitating the human voice.*

The controversies of conical *versus* cylindrical bore and wood *versus* metal for body material were finally resolved by Theobald Böhm.** Between 1831 and 1842, he perfected the modern flute which has remained essentially as he proposed.*** The body is now cylindrical (the head joint being parabolic), and although flutes of wood were still used for many years, the advantages of metal have proved to be superior. Metal**** does not crack, is not so affected by temperature and moisture, holds its pitch, and is more resonant.

Chapter IV

A STUDY OF FLUTE ARTICULATION IN THE EIGHTEENTH CENTURY

The various methods of articulation as recommended by writers in the eighteenth and early nineteenth centuries, make an interesting study. The first articulation, as advanced by Hotteterre,***** is obtained by using the syllables, *tu, ru* (See Example 1). This is nothing more than a tongued note followed by a slurred one.

---

* Longman, James, and Lukey, *Longman and Lukey's Art (in Miniature) of Blowing or Playing on ye German Flute* (London: No. 26 Cheapside, circa 1775), II, p. 4.

** See Theobald Böhm, *An Essay on the Construction of Flutes* (London: Rudall Carte & Co., 1882).

*** Interesting is the fact that as late as 1829, principles for the German flute were still set forth. See Ezekial Goodale, *The Instrumental Director* (London: Hallowell, Maine, E. Goodale, 1829), p. 6.

**** The most common metal used for the flute is silver. Other materials include gold, platinum, and nickel alloys.

***** Hotteterre-Le-Romain, *The Rudiments or Principles of the German Flute* (London: Walsh, servant to his Majesty, ((1729))), p. 17. This is a translation of Hotteterre's *Principes* of 1707. References are made to the English edition.

Example 1

From both Hotteterre and an anonymous writer * of the mid-eighteenth century, we learn that these syllables were alternated in passages, thus, slurring every other note. This pattern fits well in measures containing an uneven number of notes, but in passages of an even number, the first two would be pronounced *tu*, with alternation thereafter, as in Example 2

Apparently, the aforementioned articulation was not entirely satisfactory for around 1770, the term "double tonguing" begins to appear in treatises, and for its execution, *tootle* is suggested, as in Example 3

Although this technique is merely a method for fast tonguing, writers even into the nineteenth century recommend *tootle* or the similar *tu tel.*** Not altogether different in result from these are Quantz's use of *did'll**** and *tad'll,* suggested by Tromlitz****, as in Examples 4 and 5.

---

* *The Compleat Tutor for the German Flute* (London: Henry Waylett, circa 1745), Chapter 9.

** See *The Compleat Tutor for the German Flute* (London: C. S. Thomson, circa 1770), pp. 13-14; Granom, *opere citato,* p. 14; and Luke Heron, *A Treatise on the German Flute* (London: W. Griffin, 1771), p. 35.

*** Quantz, *opere citato,* p. 79-84. See also Gunn, *opere citato,* p. 14.

**** Tromlitz, *opere citato,* pp. 216-237.

In all of these methods, the second syllable is decidedly weaker than the first and cannot be attacked with the same clarity as the first. Perhaps the players hoped that the discrepancy would go unnoticed in rapid passages. *Did'll* is the most sluggish as the tongue, being farther back on the palate, has little force. Also, the air current through the mouth is not so well directed across the embouchure hole as with the *oo* sound of *tootle*. Although the use of *tad'll* results in a more open sound, the German flute responds too slowly for any of these methods to be executed effectively.

Methods for triple tonguing and even quadruple tonguing are mentioned in the eighteenth century. For triple tonguing, *tootle too* is employed, as in Example 6.

This is an expansion of the use of *tootle** for double tonguing. Even a method for quadruple tonguing is mentioned by Weiss, ** who says it gives a phrase more expression than double tonguing, as in Example 7.

A similar means is suggested by Tromlitz***, as in Example 8.

Both seem to be misrepresentations as the tongue is not required to speak four times, but actually, three.

The method of double tonguing in use today is an alternation of T and G or T and K. This articulation, which was already employed on other wind instruments, was not introduced for flute until the nineteenth

---

* Confer p. 7, footnote **. See also Walter Redmond, *Flute and Piccolo Tutor* (London: Francis & Day, no date).

** Charles Weiss, *A New Methodical Instruction Book for the Flute* (London: Milhouse & Son, circa 1824), p. 87.

*** Tromlitz, *loco citato*

century.* Floriant Meline** in 1821 is perhaps the first to suggest it. The objection is that it is too gutteral and ineffective. In fact Nicholson *** states that he prefers the use of *tootle*. Here, I must inform the reader why, in actual practice, the gutteral syllable K or G does not speak readily on the German flute. The small-cut embouchure hole and the fact that wood was the body material account for the problem. The frustration encountered in trying to use the modern method of tonguing could well be the reason that early writers did not advocate its use.

Another technique of articulation proposed in the eighteenth century and one also termed "double tonguing", is that of using the syllables, *ti*, *di*. In adagios and pieces containing fast repeated notes, *di* is used. An exception to this practice is the pattern of a dotted eighth note followed by a sixteenth note. In this case, *di* is used for the dotted note and *ti* for the quick note **** as in Example 9.

The alternation of the syllables *ti* and *ri* is also mentioned. According to Quantz,***** *ri* is to be pronounced sharply, thus producing the same result as *di*. The possibility that *ri* and *di* were pronounced essentially the same is supported by Lorenzoni ****** who says that *ti* and *ri* are to be alternated for dotted rhythms in adagios, as in Example 10.

Nonetheless, it seems that *di* instead of *ri* (even with rolled *r*) is the better, if either method is to be supported. Starting a note with *d* employs a broad stroke of the tongue which perhaps serves to justify its use on the notes of longer value.

---

* See Drouët, *opere citato*, p. 67; Thomas Lindsay, *The Elements of Flute-Playing* (London: The Author, 1828), p. 98; and Charles Nicholson, *Ten Perspective Lessons for the Flute* (London: Clementi & Co., circa 1821), p. 5.

** Floriant Meline, *Modern Flute Professor* (New York: The Author, 1821), p. 21.

*** Nicholson, *loco citato*.

**** Johann Samuel Petri, *Anleitung zur praktischen Musik* (Leipzig: Johann Gottlob Immanuel Breitkopf, 1782), p. 478.

***** Quantz, *opere citato*, p. 76-79.

****** Lorenzoni, *opere citato*, p. 57.

Tonguing in the low register is particularly difficult on the German flute. To ease the problem, Weiss * recommends slurring low d' rather than tonguing it. Petri ** suggests *dit ti* for the octave leap from low d', as in Example 11.

Both of these theories are sensible. Should one need to tongue a low note on the German flute, the use of the syllable beginning with *d* is practical as it uses less force of the tongue than *t*. The latter, more often than not, produces a split tone.

Because of the overall improvement of the instrument, flautists of today can make effective staccato attacks in the low register as well as the high. However, upon careful examination, it will be noted that for tonguing the former, the concept is more that of *d* than *t*.

As one ascends, the tongue moves more forward on the palate in order to keep the air column directed obliquely into the flute. According to Quantz,*** for c" and notes higher, the tongue should move between the teeth and lips so that these notes will not sound hissed. This statement has no basis. In practice, it only produces a frustrating delay in the response of the note because the tongue is in the way of the air column. Today, only amateurs are guilty of this manner of articulation. The correct way is to keep the tongue behind and above the teeth on the palate.

The portato in a modern sense of the word, denotes a compromise between staccato and legato. This articulation on repeated notes, however, seems to be the subject of controversy with the early writers. One practice is that of using a syllable beginning with *h* **** which involves releasing air from the lungs in definite pulsations, as in Example 12.

This process could not have been dependable on the early flute as the response occurs late, if at all.

---

* Weiss, *loco citato.*

** Petri, *opere citato,* p. 480.

*** Quantz, *opere citato,* p. 72.

**** See Charles de Lusse, *L'Art de la flûte traversière* (Paris: 1760), p. 8.

Lorenzoni * recommends the use of *h* for syncopation purposes, as in Example 13.

However, it is not clear whether he intends the player actually to interrupt the sound or merely to accent the note with the breath. If the latter is the case, the effect would be , a practice which reflects poor taste. This is usually associated with a beginner or someone, who in counting very hard, automatically produces a breath attack on the main beats of the measure. Other writers ** maintain that notes with dots or small vertical strokes over them contained in an arch are to be tongued. Tempo seems to be the determining factor, and it seems generally agreed upon that fast notes should be tongued.

In portato passages, accurateness is essential in order to maintain a given tempo. This can best be effected by starting each note with a soft but audible stroke of the tongue with only a minimum of space between notes. This is readily done on the flute today, but a player of the eighteenth-century flute would have had to anticipate the next note well in advance for the flute to respond on the desired beat.

An advantageous way of starting notes softly, particularly in the high register, is gained by using only the lips, similar to shaping the letter *P*. Such a process is mentioned by Longman and Lukey *** who say that use of the lips will "always occasion a wheezing." Owing again to the inferior nature of the early flute, this particular practice could not be executed effectively on the German flute. Perhaps a good solution is offered by Meline **** who suggests that the player use what seems most natural to him when the articulation is not marked.

An expression no longer in demand on the flute (except in jazz) is the glide, a gradual uncovering of the holes by moving the fingers sidewise from the holes instead of immediately up. It is discussed by Nicholson ***** who indicates it thus ⌒ , and cautions the player to let the note to which he glides be sharp as it will tend naturally to be flat. This technique is simple to execute on the German flute as the fingers come in direct contact with the tone holes. According to Ehrlich,****** the glide was used only in adagios.

---

* Lorenzoni, *loco citato.*

** See Gunn, *opere citato,* p. 13; Heron, *opere citato,* p. 18, objects to starting any note without a definite stroke of the tongue.

*** Longman and Lukey, *opere citato,* pp. 5-6.

**** Meline, *opere citato,* p. 20.

***** Nicholson, *loco citato.*

****** Ehrlich, *opere citato,* p. 64.

Chapter V

FORESHADOWINGS OF THE MODERN VIBRATO TECHNIQUE

Vibrato on the modern flute is considered a standard technique by advanced players. It heightens the emotional quality of the tone and increases the projecting power of the instrument. In reality, it is no more than a wavering of the tone best controlled from the diaphragm.* The widely accepted use of the vibrato has taken place only in the twentieth century.

De Lusse ** (1760) hints at it in presenting a unique manner of double tonguing, that of using the syllable *loul* on repeated notes of the same pitch, as in Example 14.

In practice, this produces the same effect as sending air pulsations from the diaphragm.

Mention might also be made of the softening, an ornament mentioned by writers including Hotteterre *** and Corrette. **** According to them, it is produced by lowering and raising a finger several times over a tone hole but never completely closing the hole. This results in a slight fluctuation of pitch. As it is recommended for use on long notes, one can reasonably assume that coloring the tone in this manner produced a desirable effect.

Nicholson ***** briefly discusses making vibration on the flute which is to be determined by the strength of the tone. In illustrating it, he shows the pulse slow and wide for a full sound, the speed of which gradually increases as the sound diminishes, as in Example 15.

---

* Ehrlich, *opere citato*, p. 49. suggests producing vibrato from lung pressure or trembling jaw movement.

** De Lusse, *opere citato*, p. 8.

*** Hotteterre, *opere citato*, pp. 9, 23-24.

**** See p. 43.

***** Nicholson, *loco citato*.

In an earlier treatise, * he presents two different kinds of vibration. One is described as being a modulation of the breath "bearing some similitude to a state of exhaustion or panting," and the other, a tremulous motion of the finger over the hole and marked ∿∿∿∿. The latter appears to be nothing more than a trill, but the former does bear resemblance to our modern vibrato technique. However, in order to give utmost emotion and refinement to a note marked *forte*, the player today rather uses a fast vibrato, after decreasing the speed as he diminishes the sound, as shown in Example 16.

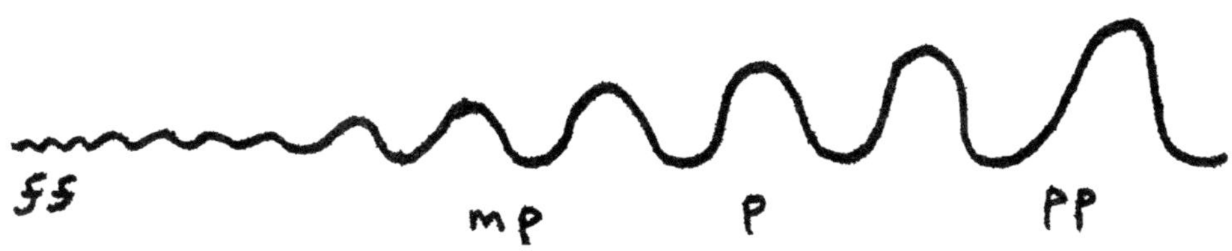

The modern principle is just the opposite of that suggested by Nicholson.

Chapter VI

CONCLUSION

Although primitive in ideas, the techniques discussed by early writers offer much information as to the nature of the flute and practices relating to it. Players in the modern age find it difficult to believe that pieces composed for the flute in the eighteenth century were performed on an instrument with more imperfections than merits.

It would be frustrating indeed to attempt performance on the flute today using principles set forth for the German flute. Solos, as well as chamber and orchestral works, require a flute of brilliance and strength. The early flute would not lend itself for modern practices such as fluttertonguing, slapping the keys for percussive effect, and playing two harmonic pitches simultaneously. Nor could it be capable of sounding well in today's orchestra of great depths and contrasts.

Could we have heard the early virtuosos on the flute in view of present standards, we might find the playing intolerable. And then again, credit should be given to anyone who played on the German flute that rather hindered good playing than promoted it.

---

* Charles Nicholson, *Nicholson's Complete Preceptor for the German Flute* (London: Preston, 1816), p. 23.

Chapter VII

MICHEL CORRETTE

Michel Corrette (1709-1795), a French organist and composer, is the author of a vocal method and of treatises for several instruments, including the oboe, violin, violoncello, harpsichord, hurdy-gurdy, and flute. The dating of the last-named work is controversial. François J. Fétis * dates it 1778 and a second edition 1781; Eugene Borrel ** says it was first written in 1753; according to Robert Eitner, *** the flute treatise was written in 1710.

Evidence, however, that 1741 is a *terminus ad quem* is the fact that it is listed in a catalogue of Corrette's works in his *Methode, theorique et practique pour apprendre... le violoncelle dans sa perfection* (Paris: 1741). Other evidence, which serves to establish a *terminus a quo* may be found in the music. A specific example is a minuet **** excerpted from *Dardanus*, ***** a *tragédie-lyrique* by Jean-Philippe Rameau which was first presented in 1739. The opera was revised in 1744, but this particular minuet is found in the 1739 version. Corrette shows a gavotte ****** which he claims is also from *Dardanus*, ******* but if this is so, it is not found in any published version. Other music and the composers to whom Corrette refers throughout his treatise were known before he wrote his flute method. ********

An examination of the internal content of the treatise certainly places it before the middle of the eighteenth century. The flute that Corrette discusses is the German flute with only the key for D♯. He mentions nothing of additional keys as do writers of a slightly later period.*********

---

* François J. Fétis, "Corrette, Michel," in the *Biographie universelle des musiciens et bibliographie générale de la musique* (second edition; Paris: 1875). Reprinted (Brussel/Bruxelles: 1963), II, p. 356.

** Eugène Borrel, "Corrette, Michel," in *Die Musik in Geschichte und Gegenwart* (Kassel: Bärenreiter, 1952), II, column 1695.

*** Robert Eitner, "Corrette, Michel," in the *Biographisch-bibliographische Quellen-Lexikon der Musiker und Musikgelehrten...* (Leipzig: Breitkopf & Härtel, 1900-1904), III-IV, p. 64.

**** See p. 54.

***** Jean-Philippe Rameau, *Oeuvres complètes*, ed. Camille Saint-Saëns. 18 Vols. (Paris: Durand, 1895-1924), X.

****** See p. 52.

******* There is another *Dardanus*, an opera by Antonio Maria Gaspare Sacchini dated 1784, but the Gavotte is not found there. Nor is it likely to be found in Karl Stamitz' opera of the same title.

******** Confer pp. 23, 27, 31, 34, 50, 53, and 62.

********* See Heron, *opere citato*, p. 19; Petri, *opere citato*, p. 360; *Compleat Tutor* (circa 1770), p. 14.

Although brief, Corrette's treatment of articulation is interesting in that he states that the syllables *tu* and *ru* * are outmoded. However, as he does not present any other method, it may be assumed that he alludes to the various kinds of double tonguing that begin to appear around the middle of the century.

Still another indication that Corrette's treatise is early is exemplified in the fingering chart which shows fingerings for notes between d' and a'''. ** De Lusse (1760) *** is one of the first writers to offer fingerings for higher notes.

The present translation of Corrette's flute method is an attempt to contribute to the literature on the eighteenth-century flute. An endeavor has been made to find a satisfactory compromise between a literal and liberal translation. When there appears to be ambiguity, the translator has explained the original word or phrase in a footnote. Corrette's importance has yet to be fully evaluated, but it is significant that his flute method is the first independent one to be known after Hotteterre's *Principes* of 1707. **** It is believed that the English translation of Hotteterre's work was made circa 1729, which is unmistakably plagiarized in Peter Prelleur's *Modern Musick-Master* of 1730. The anonymous tutors that began to appear shortly after this date are only adaptations of this.

Corrette is not always consistent in his text; for example, he sometimes spells out his words "sharp", "flat", and "natural", and at other times he merely uses signs for them. Also inconsistent is his capitalization of substantives, such as minuet, saraband, sonata, concerto, etc. For uniformity, the translator has used signs and minuscules throughout the work. However, for the terms "Allegro" and "Adagio" which Corrette applies generically to fast and slow pieces, majuscules will be retained.

Another problem arises from Corrette's system of naming the notes, which he does in three ways. First, he identifies the syllables, ut, re, mi, fa, sol, la, si, with respective notes; he then lists names of the notes familiar to us, i.e., C, D, E, F, G, A, B; and finally, he uses letters in alphabetical order for examples, A, B, C, D, etc. To overcome and hopefully simplify all of this, the translator has chosen to retain the use of "French" syllables where Corrette applies them, to use cursive majuscules for the names that he shows, and to use Roman *capitalis* for his examples as they occur in alphabetical order

Footnotes found in the text are those of Corrette. Those of the translator are placed at the bottom of the pages.

---

* See p. 34, and Hotteterre, *opere citato*, p. 17.

** See pp. 32-33.

*** De Lusse, *opere citato*, p. 5.

**** There is record of an obscure work by Johann Christian Schickhard, *Flötenschule*, opus 12, Amsterdam. Although not dated, it could possibly have preceded Corrette's work.

METHOD FOR EASILY LEARNING TO PLAY ON THE TRANSVERSE FLUTE

With Principles of Music and Pieces for

Parts I and II

Useful and curious work which guides in very little time to the perfect knowledge of music and playing sonatas and concertos at sight.

By Mr. Corrette

Paris

At Mr. Boivin, rue St. Honore à la Regle d'Or
Clerk, rue du Roule à la Croix d'Or

Lyons

Mr. de Bretonne, rue Merciere

With Consent of the King

PREFACE

The method embodies not only the true manner to learn the first elements of the transverse flute, but also several notes and ornaments of which earlier methods have not spoken, and at the same time most of the notes and ornaments of these methods teach bad fingerings which hinder true playing

I therefore thought to please the public in sharing the discoveries that the great masters have made on this fine instrument. At the same time ((I)) assure those who learn by this method that they will never be wrong in making accurate notes, trills, softenings, beats, and all the ornaments of the most clarity with accurate rules for making them when they are not marked in the music

We also give here some principles of music useful for the flute with airs known for their simplicity for students, preludes, with the art of improvising, and the way of knowing the sensitive notes and tones of a piece.

Finally, all that which is believed to be necessary for beginning, and worthy of the curiosity of people already advanced in the art of playing the flute, will be found in this method.

NOTE

In the beginning, one must avoid as much as possible making music with bagpipes and hurdy-gurdies. These types of instruments are of a limited modulation, hurt the ear, are never in tune, and always make bad dissonances.* Most of all, do not play in C, which is the deafest key of the flute.**

---

* This is a curious statement as Corrette, in his *La Belle Vielleuse, Methode pour apprendre facilement a jouer de la vielle* (Paris: Chez les Marchands assortis, ((circa 1780))), p. 1, says that the "hurdy-gurdy is a pleasing and brilliant instrument." Hotteterre-Le-Romain, *Methode pour la musette* (Paris: J.-B.-Christophe Ballard, 1735), p. iii, states that "of all instruments, the bagpipe is the most pleasing."

** Perhaps Corrette means that because the flute is tuned in the key of C (non-transposing), this key is the least interesting. Nicholson, in his *Ten Perspective Lessons...*, p. 73, states that "B major is the sweetest key on the instrument."

Which of the two here is the teacher ((?))

This book now acquired, may disappear.

Method for Easily Learning to Play on the Transverse Flute

Chapter I

PRINCIPLES OF MUSIC FOR THE FLUTE

The eight notes, of which the last is only a repetition of the first, compose the scale of music designated as the octave. In ascending order, the degrees are named: ut, ré, mi, fa, sol, la, si, ut; and descending: ut, si, la, sol, fa, mi, ré, ut.

G-clef on the second line:

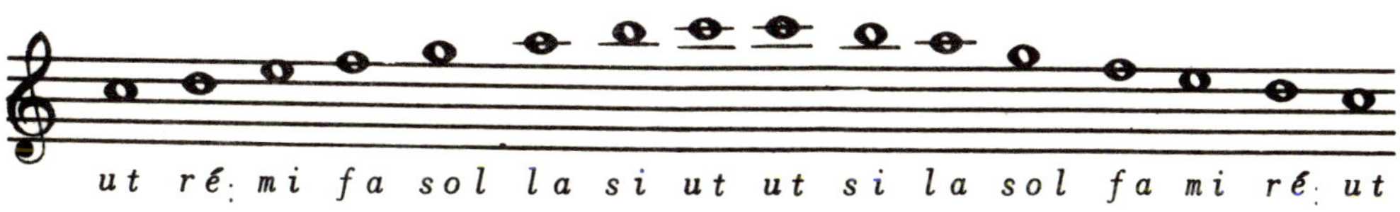

Range of the transverse flute

G-clef on the first line:

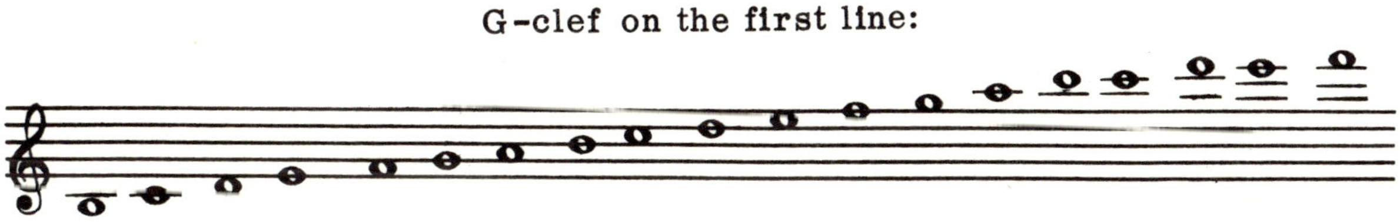

The lines above and below the five are added to fill out the range of the flute, which is a nineteenth. Foreigners * rarely play music when the G-clef is placed on the first line. ** They believe that music written in this clef is not good. Thus, all the examples and lessons contained in this method are in the G-clef placed on the second line.

---

* I.e., nationalities other than the French.

** The G-clef on the first line designated use of the recorder and was used in French music until about the middle of the eighteenth century.

Chapter II

VALUES OF THE NOTES AND RESTS

The method is in the clef placed on the second line:

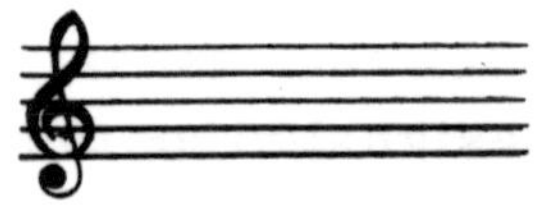

The notes are divided into whole, half, quarter, eighth, sixteenth, thirty-second, etc.

The whole is the longest of all.

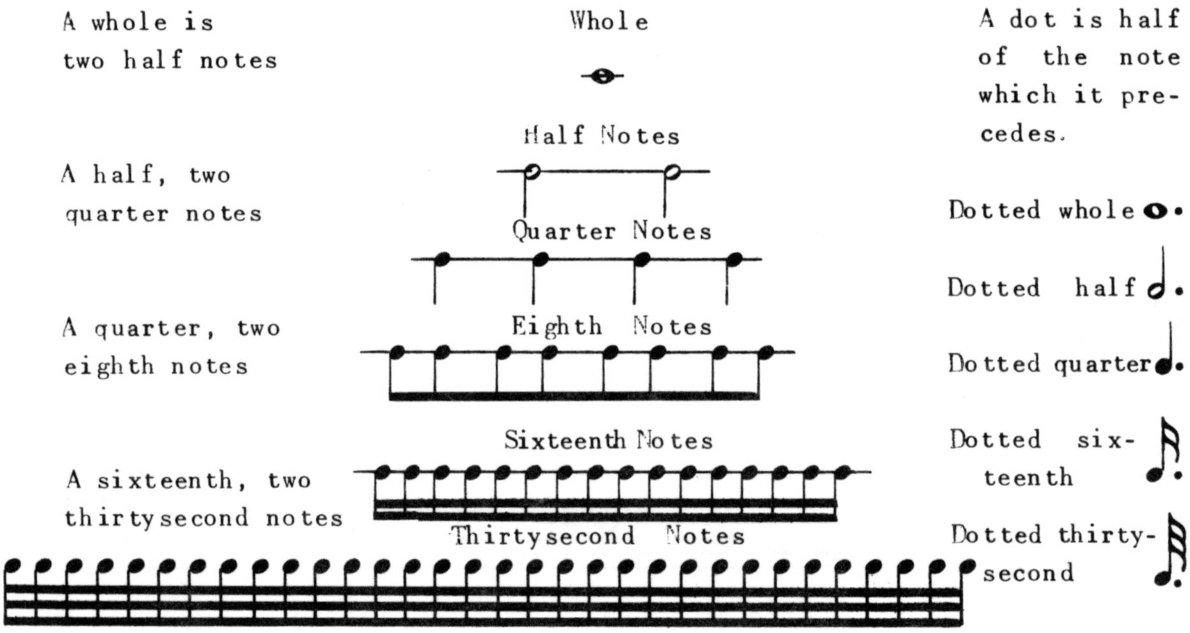

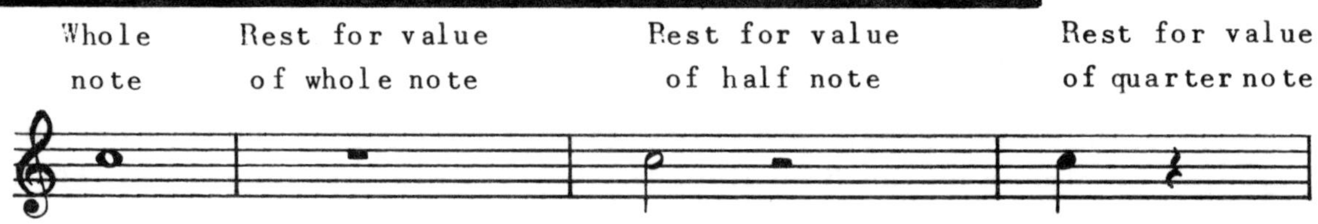

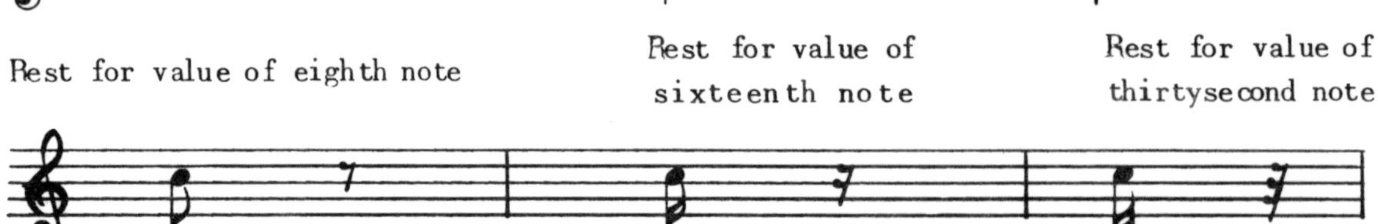

Manner of showing rests for one or several measures.*

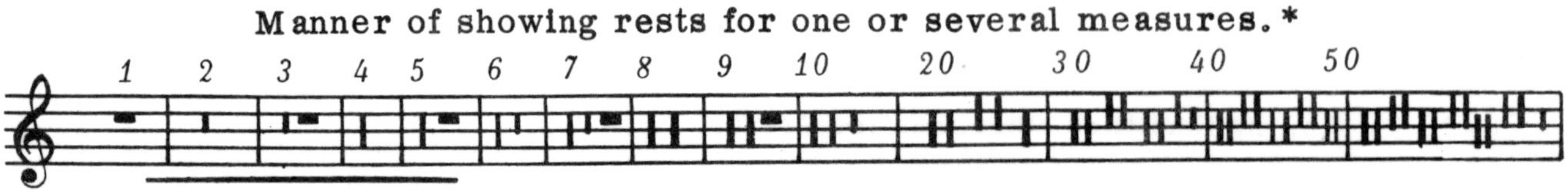

* This method of indicating rests was carried over from earlier notational practices.

Chapter III

THE SHARPS (♯), FLATS (♭), AND NATURALS (♮)

There are three signs for changing the notes. Observe: the sharp, ♯, which raises the note a semitone, the flat, ♭, which lowers the note a semitone, and the natural, ♮, which renders the note in its natural state.

The sharps and flats beside the clef affect all the notes which are placed on the same lines ((and spaces)) and for those at the octave above and below.

Chapter IV

THE SIGNS EMPLOYED IN MUSIC

The bar (|) serves to enclose the measure. The double bars with dots (:||) or (:||:) mark the middle of the piece or the end. It is necessary that each section be played two times.

The return sign (𝄋) indicates that one must begin at the place where the same sign is found.

The custos (𝆘) is placed at the end of the lines to show where the note is found on the following line.

The tie ⌒ or syncopation sign indicates that two notes must be kept with the same tongue attack.

Syncopation

The slurs ⌒⌒ above or below show all notes that are made in the same attack of the tongue.*

Slurs

---

* See p. 34.

Chapter V

CONCERNING THE MEASURE

The movement of a piece is marked by numbers except $\frac{4}{4}$ time which is marked by C or ¢. All the different ways of indicating the meter in music may be reduced to two or three time signatures. The others have only been thought of for marking more precisely the degree of speed or slowness.

The meter $\frac{4}{4}$ time contains twice the number of beats as $\frac{2}{4}$ time. Also, the accents of the two ways differ. Observe that in allegros there is one beat, and in adagios or other slow parts, two beats if necessary. In $\frac{4}{4}$ and $\frac{12}{8}$ time, one can have two accents.

$\frac{4}{4}$ time, C or ¢, is often found in Italian music, such as in the Allemande, Adagio, Allegro, and Presto of sonatas and concertos.

One must play eighth notes equal and play the sixteenth notes unequal in pairs.* One can also play them equal in Allegros and Prestos of sonatas and concertos.

2 marks the beat in $\frac{2}{4}$ time. This meter is used in Rigaudons, Gavottes, Bourées, and Cotillons in French music. The Italians hardly use these at all. It must be pointed out that to play the eighth notes in pairs, one makes the first one long and the second one short ((sometimes)).**

3 marks the measure in three beats. This meter is used for Minuets, Sarabands, Courants, Chaconnes, etc. The Italians always mark this meter $\frac{3}{4}$ as in the composite signs.***

Meters in two beats	Meters in three beats	Meters in two unequal beats****	Meter in four beats
$\frac{2}{4}$ $\frac{2}{8}$ $\frac{2}{6}$	$\frac{3}{4}$ $\frac{3}{2}$ $\frac{3}{8}$ $\frac{3}{9}$	$\frac{6}{4}$	$\frac{12}{8}$

$\frac{2}{4}$ or $\frac{2}{8}$ is duple mater for the Italians. This meter is often used in Allegros and Prestos of sonatas and concertos. The eighth notes must be played equal and the sixteenth notes unequal. One sometimes also plays them equally in sonatas.

$\frac{6}{8}$ is used in the French and Italian Gigues. One plays the eighth notes equal. One often slurs the first two and sometimes three.

---

* Jean-Jacques Rousseau, *Dictionaire de Musique* (Paris: Duchesne, 1768), trans. William Waring (London: 1779), p. 321. In French music, all eighth notes are played unequal, except in $\frac{4}{4}$ time. In all the rest, they are pointed (dotted) unless marked otherwise. The resulting rhythmic pattern is . In Italian music, all eighth notes are played equal unless dotted in music. A study of the French *inégales* (beyond the scope of this book) may be found in Robert Donnington, *The Interpretation of Early Music* (London: Faber and Faber, 1963) and Arnold Dolmetsch, *The Interpretation of the Music of the Seventeenth and Eighteenth Centuries* (London: Novello & Co., Ltd., 1944).

** The word "sometimes" appears inserted by hand in a later copy of this work.

*** Sébastian de Brossard, *Dictionaire de musique* (Paris: Christophe Ballard, 1705). In the article, "Menuet", he says that the Italians' use of $\frac{3}{4}$ signature should be imitated, but the custom of marking it by 3 prevails.

**** I.e., two groups of three beats.

$\frac{3}{2}$ indicates a slow movement. This meter is often used in the Saraband.

It must be pointed out that the quarter notes in pairs are sometimes played equal according to the character of the piece, as in the English air, "Dultymiller". See *Chansons angloises* arranged for the flute by Mr. Corrette.*

$\frac{3}{8}$ is used in the French Passepieds.** This meter in three beats is very often found in the Affetuosos, Minuets, and Allegros of sonatas. One must play the eighth and sixteenth notes equal.

$\frac{9}{8}$ is rarely found in French music but quite often in Italian music, such as in the Gigue, Allegro, and Presto. The eighth notes are played equal, but the sixteenth notes must be played unequal.

$\frac{6}{4}$ is a meter of two uneven beats. This is used for the Loure in French music. The English compose many Vaudevilles and Country Dances in this meter. See "Bartholomew Fair," "Hunt the Squirrel," "Lillibulero," and "Hooptpettycoat" in the *Chansons angloises*.***

These airs are to be played in a noble manner, showing well the quarter notes and dotting the eighth notes in pairs. This meter is found very little in Italian music.

$\frac{12}{8}$ is found in Italian, German, French, and English music. One must play the eighth notes equal and the sixteenth notes unequal.

Quite often one takes the first two and sometimes three eighth notes in one attack of the tongue.

Pieces rarely change in time**** except the overture, of which the beginning is in time, and the recapitulation occurs in one of the meters above.***** The beat is marked with the foot.******

Those who wish to know the duration of a rest or a note held can see the chronometer of Mr. Loulié ******* or Mr. Sauveur. See the

---

* In the catalogue of Corrette's works found in his violoncello method, there is the entry *Chansons angloises accomodis pour deux flutes*. However, this work does not seem to have survived. The tune "Dultymiller" could be a misspelling of "The Dusty Miller", a tune which is discussed in William Chappell, *Popular Music of the Olden Time* (New York: Dover, 1965), II, p. 608.

** See also Johann Sebastian Bach, "English Suite", No. V.

*** For the tunes "Bartholomew Fair" and "Lillibulero", see Chappell, *opere citato*, pp. 585 and 568. "Lillibulero" was used as a political tune in the seventeenth century. It also appears as a ground in *The Gordian Knot Unty'd* by Henry Purcell (see Willi Apel, *Harvard Dictionary of Music* Cambridge, Massachusetts: Harvard University Press, 1961).

**** *Mouvement*.

***** See the overture to *Armide* by Lully. It begins in $\frac{2}{2}$ time and changes to $\frac{6}{4}$.

****** In an amusing way, writers (including the anonymous ones) mention beating of time with one's foot.

******* Étienne Loulié was the first to use the chronometer to beat time. See his *Elements ou principes de musique... avec l'estampie et l'usage du chronometre* (Paris:. 1696). trans. Albert Cohen (New York: Institute of Mediaeval Music, Ltd., 1965). References are made to the English edition.

Memoires de l'Academie royale des Sciences, 1701. The performer can easily learn harmony.

OBSERVATION

The number 3 above three notes means to play them in the same time as one plays two notes, *A*. The 6 above or below six notes means that these should be played in the duration of four notes, *B*. These are found in sonatas of modern composers.

Example

Method for the Flute

Chapter I

CONCERNING THE COMPOSITION OF THE TRANSVERSE FLUTE

The transverse flute, called by some the German flute, and by the Italians *flauto,* is ordinarily made of box-wood or plum wood, grenadille, maple wood, black ebony, lighter ebony, etc.*

They are often made with visible trim of ivory, brass, silver, even of gold, but these have nothing to do with the quality of the instrument.**

The most modern flutes are made in four parts and are easily carried in the pocket. Formerly, they were made in three parts which were inconvenient to carry.***

The first part is called the head. In this piece is pierced a hole which serves as the mouthpiece of the flute. In the second part, called first body, are pierced three holes which the left hand covers. In the third piece, named second body, are also pierced three holes which the right hand covers. And in the fourth part, called foot, is pierced one hole which is always closed by a key of brass or silver. This key, of course, closes the hole which in turn is opened by pressing the key with the small finger of the right hand.

---

* Confer p. 3.

** William Bainbridge, *Observations on the Cause of Imperfections on Wind Instruments, Particularly in German Flutes* (London: J. Innes, 1823), in his Introduction, comments that too many flutes are made to please the eye and not the ear.

*** Confer p. 3. Corrette seems to be the first writer to mention the extra middle pieces. In his earlier treatise, Hotteterre makes no mention of them.

All flutes have the pitch for opera, but it is often found that in harmony with the harpsichord, they are too high or too low. Ordinarily, there are several replacement parts of different lengths to match the pitch of the harpsichord. This changing of parts is only for the first. Indeed, such variations in pitch are hardly corrected before some singer capriciously gives himself an air or the singers * have colds. Nonetheless, the body replacements are very useful.

All the world knows of this instrument which is adapted to play the treble. The G-clef is ordinarily found on the second line for concertos and sonatas. In French opera music, the clef is on the first line. **

Chapter II

CONCERNING THE MANNER OF HOLDING THE TRANSVERSE FLUTE

In order to play the transverse flute, it is necessary to hold the body correctly, the head of the flute higher than the foot joint, turning toward the left shoulder. ***

It is necessary to hold the flute with both hands, the left hand above, *A*, and the right hand below, *B*. See the illustration. The left hand should support this instrument between the thumb and first finger and bend the wrist a little downwards; but one must hold it so that the first and second fingers are arched and the third a little extended toward the right hand.

The little finger of the left hand does not serve a function but is held a little in the air.

For the right hand, one must have the thumb support the flute, the other fingers, instead of holding the instrument, are all needed to cover the holes, with regard to the notes which will be explained in Chapter IV. **** The thumb of the right hand should be underneath the fourth hole of the flute, a little further down, if one wishes; the first, second, and third fingers more straight than arched; but the little finger well extended so that it will always be ready to press down the key, *D*, the wrist flexed a little inward.

None of the fingers of the left and right hands ever changes place, but when the holes are uncovered, they are simply held above. It is necessary that one take caution not to hold them so high that they retard execution.

---

* *Elles*. Corrette's remark is witty but caustic about the tempramental nature associated with singers.

** See p. 19, footnote **.

*** The practice of turning toward the left shoulder was customary. See Hotteterre, *opere citato*, p. 1; Heron, *opere citato*, p. 18; and Devienne, *opere citato*, p. 2.

**** See pp. 27 ff.

One must, by all means, observe not to make grimaces or to have ridiculous posture. The flute, being a noble instrument, is to be played in a relaxed manner. One can play standing or seated, depending on the occasion, but when one plays the first movement of a solo concerto or sonata, or accompanies a cantata by score, one plays better when standing. The instrument is heard better.

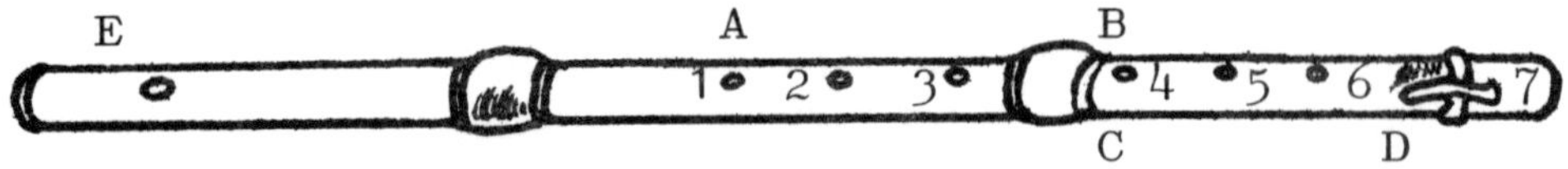

Chapter III

CONCERNING THE MANNER OF FORMING THE EMBOUCHURE

The embouchure is very difficult on the flute, but one can acquire it in very little time, by following the way we are about to give here.

1. It is necessary to place the lips on the embouchure hole, *E* (see the figure of the flute above), joining them together, and make a small opening in the middle for the passage of air. And to form it easily, one must tighten the lips in the corners of the mouth, and place the embouchure hole of the flute towards the small opening; then press the air out very gently.*

2. There are some who can only play the flute by advancing the lower lip on the hole.** For the rest, one cannot give any rule which does not have some exception. This depends on the placement of the lips, but the principle of the mouth formation is to make the flute ring and have a clear sound. In the beginning, it is necessary that one exercise to acquire the embouchure. There are some people who have it naturally, because ((to them)) the embouchure of the flute is not more difficult than blowing in a key hole.

3. One can turn the flute a little inward or outward to make the blowing easier. After one has learned the embouchure of the flute, he must learn the first octave, ré, mi, fa, sol, la, si, ut♯, ré. Observe that I sharpen the article ut. It is not that one cannot play ut♮, but in the beginning it is better to sharpen ut which is the leading tone of the ré scale. That sharpens the ear at the true modulation, but we shall speak more of the leading tone in Chapter XIII, p. 45.*** It is necessary in making ré to cover all the holes and to blow very gently. This tone is difficult to make because all of the holes must be well covered. But one shouldn't try too hard in the beginning; usage overcomes this difficulty.

---

* Longman and Lukey, *opere citato*, pp. 5-6, "... the stronger you press your lips to the Flute, and the more steadily it is held, the more sweet the tone and less the fatigue."

** Quantz, *opere citato*, p. 52, advises people with unusually thick lips to play a little to the left rather than in the middle of the lips". Nicholson, *opere citato* , p.4, even says that the orifice should be formed from the soft or innermost part of the lips.

*** See p. 56.

One must yet observe, the degree at which the notes rise, one must increase the wind, but with imperceptible graduation for the first octave: ré, mi, fa, sol, la, si, ut, ré. But to make the higher notes, one must give a little more air, always saving it, not making it so loud that the tone shakes. *

The fife only differs from the German flute in that it speaks louder, tones are more shrill and brilliant, and it is shorter and narrower. The Swiss like this instrument very much. **

At the present time in Paris, small transverse flutes at the octave are being made which render a charming effect in Tambourines and concertos made especially for the flute. *** See the works of Messieurs Boismortier, Corrette, Nodeau, **** Braun, and Quantz. *****

Chapter IV

CONCERNING THE RANGE OF THE TRANSVERSE FLUTE AND THE FINGERS THAT MUST BE EMPLOYED TO MAKE EACH TONE AND SEMITONE

Here is the way to make the tones and semitones according to the very skillful masters of Paris and foreign countries, and in order to make it easier, I am going to demonstrate two different ways by two tables.

---

* Quantz, *opere citato*, p. 54, says that in producing higher tones, "on no account must the wind be increased or doubled". ((Jacques de)) Vaucanson, *An Account of the Mechanism of the Automation, or Image playing on the German Flute* (London: T. Parker, 1742), p. 6, states that the wind force must be increased for higher notes.

** This is taken almost verbatim from Mersenne, *opere citato*, p. 312.

*** The small transverse flute is described in the *Kurtzgefasste musicalische Lexicon* (Chemnitz: Johann Christoph & Johann David Stősseln, 1737), p. 144, 23 sounding two octaves higher than the horn. Garsault, *opere citato*, p. 636, states that the piccolo has the same fingerings as the flute, is shorter and thinner than the flute, and sounds an octave higher. Both instruments are used to accompany dances and the piccolo for imitating bird calls. The piccolo referred to in these texts is a type of recorder, not the modern-day piccolo.

**** It is most probable that Corrette has misspelled the name Jean-Jacques Naudot, a composer and one of the first artists to distinguish himself on the transverse flute. According to Fétis, *opere citato*, VI, p. 285, Naudot was in Paris between 1720 and 1726.

***** Each of these men composed for the flute and/or was a flautist himself. Joseph Bodin de Boismortier wrote vocal and instrumental works, including some for flute. His Concertos for five flutes are still performed today. Corrette composed solo and chamber works for the flute. Braun, a German musician known as "Braun le Cadet", was in Paris circa 1740 and was considered a flautist of merit. Quantz was a prolific composer for flute and a renowned performer on that instrument. As already noted, he visited Paris in 1726. In a seemingly later edition of Corrette's flute treatise, he lists Abinnoni ((sic)), Schickhard, Nodeau, Baustetetter (i.e., Bau-stetter), Quantz, and Chinzer.

The first explains that for each tone and semitone, the fingers must cover or uncover the seven holes on the flute, and the majuscules refer to the written note at the beginning of the first table. Observe that once the note is sharpened, it never changes, neither on the instrument nor in the music. For example, the sol placed on the line in the G-clef is always made with the three fingers of the left hand, while the fingers of the right hand are raised. The la at the top of the G-clef is always played with the first and second fingers of the left hand, all the others raised. Like this, the other ⟪fingerings⟫ will be demonstrated accordingly.

One can, nevertheless, learn the tones and semitones by the black and white circles written under the notes in the second table on the seven lines representing the seven holes on the flute.* The black circles (●) represent the holes which must be covered, and the white circles (○), those which are uncovered. This is to say, do not take the fingers down.

Thus, one lowers all the fingers over the holes in closing them, except the little finger of the right hand, which must be held above the key to close the hole which is under it.

On each note represented in the following two tables is written the name above the note for the convenience of beginning, and the majuscules below the notes show the way which helps foreigners in learning them.

According to the ancient system of St. Gregory, who began on *A* mi la, thereafter, the other tones follow the order of the first seven letters of the alphabet.**

Example

Names of the notes to foreigners: *A*, *B*, *C*, *D*, *E*, *F*, *G*.
Names in French: la, si, ut, ré, mi, fa, sol.

One begins again on la into infinity for all the rest of the octaves.

It is easy to see by this example that *A* means to say la, *B* si, *C* ut, *D* ré, *E* mi, *F* fa, *G* sol, etc.

Names of the Fingers and Manner of Counting Them on the Flute

Left Hand			Right Hand			
1	2	3	4	5	6	7
index	middle	ring finger	index	middle	ring finger	little finger

I marked all the sharps with half notes 𝅗𝅥 to distinguish them from the natural notes which I marked with the whole note 𝅝 . When in the middle of a piece one needs to know how to finger a tone or a semitone, he will have the following tables to which he can turn.

---

* See pp. 32-33.

** It was Guido rather than St. Gregory who assigned these syllables to the notes. See J. Smits van Waesberghe (ed.), *Guidonis Aretini Micrologus* (Roma: American Institute of Musicology, 1955).

In the beginning, one may content oneself to learn the natural notes, and then the sharps and flats in proportion to the extent that they are found in a piece. Otherwise, one can learn at one time all the naturals and semitones. That goes to the discretion of the teacher.

FIRST TABLE

Here is explained the fingers which are necessary to make each tone and semitone.

G-clef on the second line:

First Octave

To make ré♮, *(A)*, at the bottom of the clef, cover all the holes.
For ré♯, press the key with the little finger.
For mi♮, *(B)*, cover first, second, third, fourth, fifth, and seventh holes.
For fa♮, *(C)*, cover first, second, third, fourth, sixth, and seventh holes.
For fa♯, cover first, second, third, and fourth holes.
For sol♮, *(D)*, it is only necessary to cover the first three holes.
For sol♯, cover all except the third hole.
For la♮, *(E)*, cover only the first two holes.
For la♯, cover first, third, fourth, fifth, and seventh holes.
For si♮, *(F)*, cover the first hole.
For ut♮, *(G)*, cover second and third holes.
For ut♯, uncover all the holes.

Second Octave

To make the tones and semitones of this octave, one must blow a little harder.*

---

* Confer p. 27.

For ré above the G-clef, *(H)*, cover all but the first hole

Observe that these notes are fingered like those of the octave below.

For ré♯, all holes covered except the seventh.
For mi♮, *(I)*, all holes covered except the sixth.
For fa♮, *(K)*, all holes covered except the fifth.
For fa♯, the first four holes covered.
For sol♮, *(L)*, the first three holes covered.
For sol♯, first, second, fourth, and sixth holes covered.
For la♮, *(M)*, first two holes covered like la in the octave below.

For si♮, *(N)*, first hole covered like in the octave below.
For ut♮, *(O)*, second, fourth, fifth, and sixth holes covered.
For ut♯, second, third, and fourth holes covered. One can also make ut♯ by preparing the trill of si quickly, uncovering all the holes.

Third Octave

It is necessary to tighten the lips to make the high notes.

For ré♮, *(P)*, second and third holes covered.
For ré♯, first, second, third, fifth, and sixth holes covered.
For mi♮, *(Q)*, first, second, fifth, and sixth holes covered.
For fa♮, *(R)*, first, second, third, fourth, fifth, and seventh holes covered.
For fa♯, first, third, fourth, fifth, and seventh holes covered.
For sol♮, *(S)*, third and seventh holes covered.

Notes which former players never used on the flute: *

For sol♯, third hole covered.
For la♮, *(T)*, second, third, fourth, fifth, and seventh holes covered.

These tones are rarely used in improvising. **

---

* Corrette is possibly referring to Hotteterre, *opere citato*, p. 3, who states that the notes from e‴ and above are forced and seldom used.

** Generally these high notes were avoided as they were hard to produce and intonation was poor. See the preludes pp. 57-60.

Observation of the Sharps and Flats

It is easy to see in the above table, that ré to mi is a tone, while ré♯ is in the middle which cuts the tone in half, and ré♯ is the same as mi ♭. It is true that ré♯ and mi b have some small difference, but it is so small a thing, that one need not spend time looking for this on the flute.*

Thus, the same holes which will be covered or uncovered to make the sharps of ut♯, ré♯, fa♯, sol♯, and la♯, serve also to make the flats of mi♭, sol♭, la♭, si♭, and ré♭ ((respectively)).

Ré♯ is the same as mi♭, which is a semitone between ré♮ and mi♮.
Fa♯ is the same as sol♭, which is a semitone between fa♮ and sol♮.
Sol♯ is the same as la♭, which is a semitone between sol♮ and la♮.
La♯ is the same as si♭, which is a semitone between la♮ and si♮.
And ut♯ is the same as ré♭, which is a semitone between ut♮ and ré♮.

In observing if the notes are in the second or third octave: for example, la♭ of the first octave is fingered like sol♯ of the same octave, and la♭ of the second octave like sol♯ of the same octave, the same of the others.

The tone is composed of two semitones, one major and the other minor. The major one is composed of five commas and the minor one of four; thus, it takes nine commas for a tone.** But on the flute and other instruments, the tone is only divided into semitones.

In the second table, I have made the sharps ascending and the flats descending in order to make things more logical to the student.

Observations on mi♯, si♯, and fax

Mi♯ is made like fa♮.
Si♯ is like ut♮.
Fax is like sol♮.

The last is rarely found. See *Cantate d'Orphée* by Mr. Clérambault.***

---

* It is precisely for this small difference that Quantz added the second D♯ or E♭ key. See Badger, *opere citato*, p. 8 and Quantz, *opere citato*, p. 46.

** The mean-tone temprament, which produced d discrepancy of nearly a quarter-tone between enharmonic sharps and flats, was the harmonic system used in France at this time. Equal temprament was not established until the nineteenth century. See James M. Barbour, *Tuning and Temprament* (East Lansing: Michigan State College Press, 1953). See also Quantz, *opere citato*, p. 46 and pp. 267-268 for tuning and pitch.

*** See the flute part of Nicolas Clérambault's *Orphée* in *Cantates françoises* (Paris: Bureau d'Édition de la Schola Cantorum, 1710).

SECOND TABLE OR SCALE OF ALL THE TONES AND SEMITONES OF THE TRANSVERSE FLUTE

The figures on the seven lines show the fingers of which we speak in the chart.

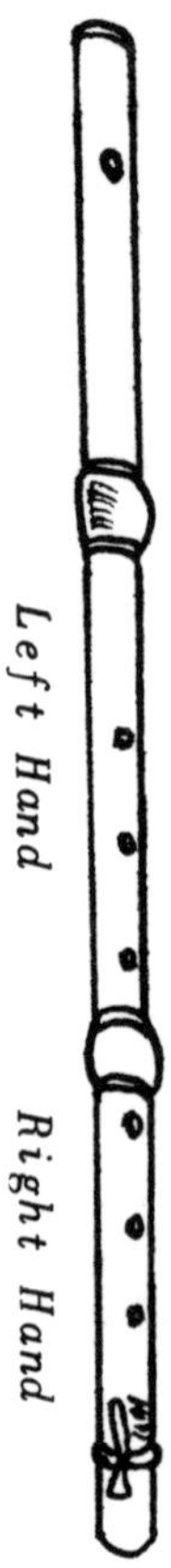

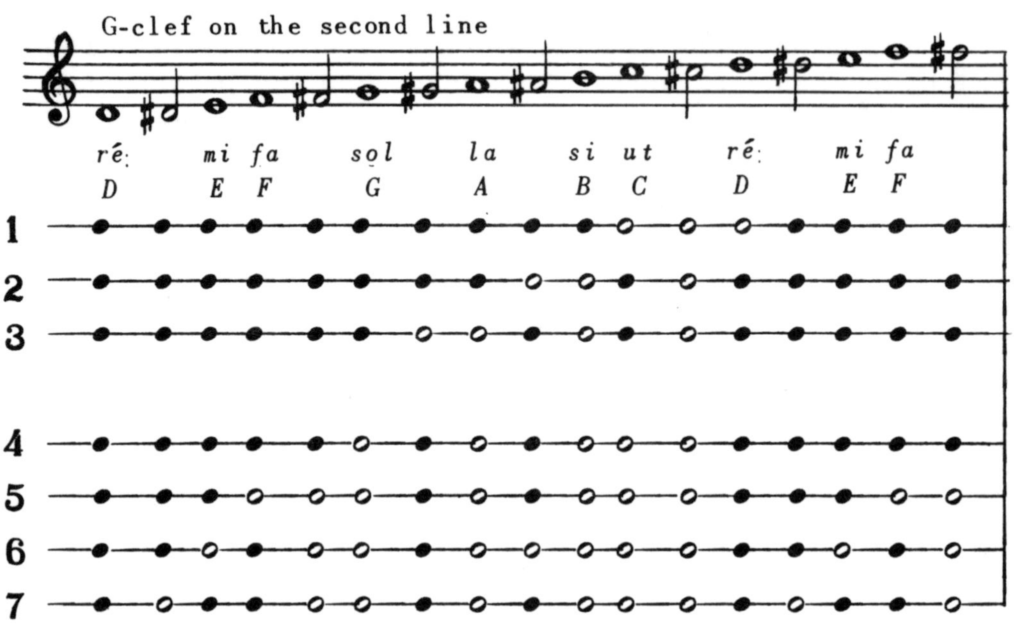

You find that to close the seventh hole, one does not press the key, *A*, with the little finger, but rather, leaves it off.

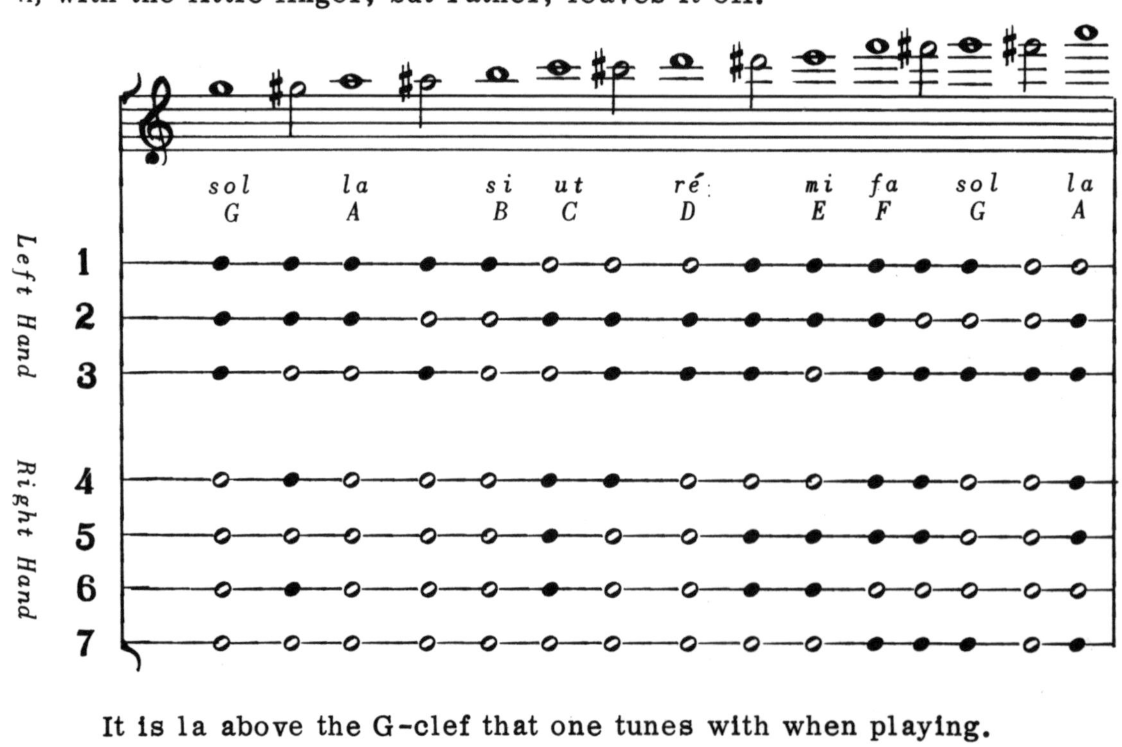

It is la above the G-clef that one tunes with when playing.

In descending, the sharps become flats.

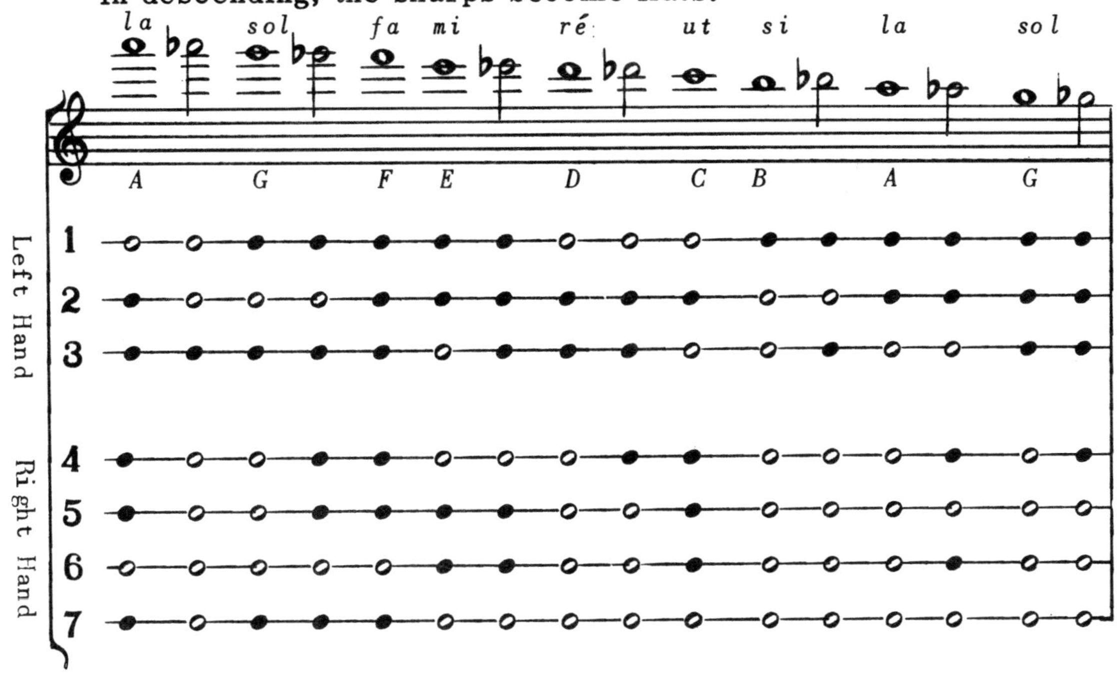

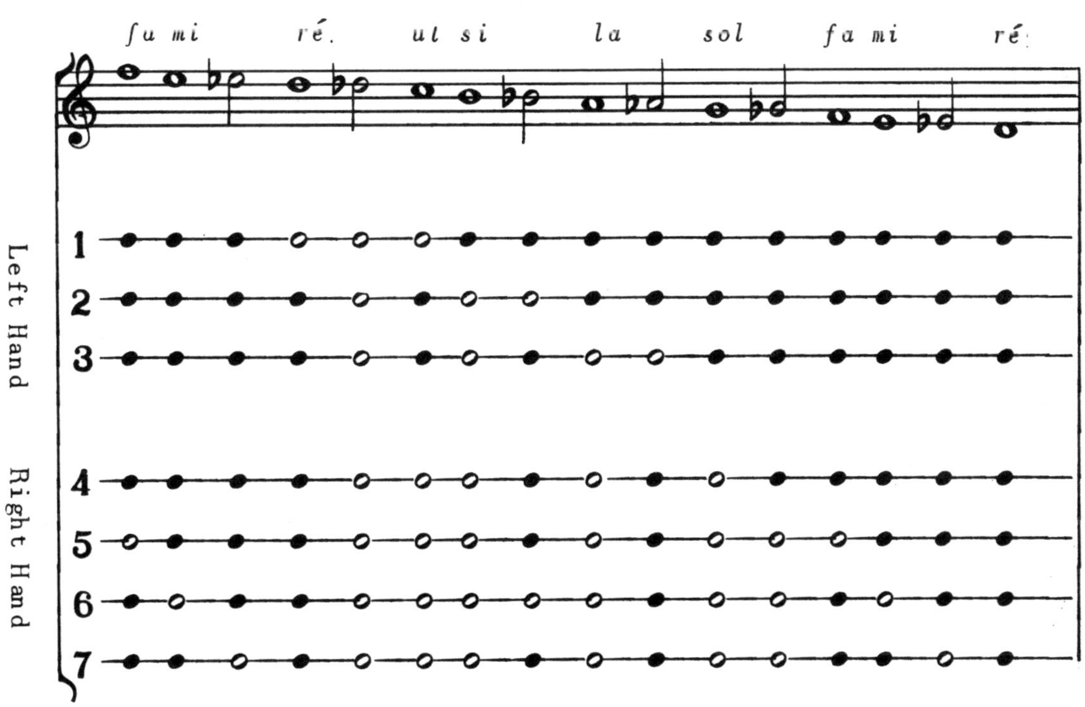

Chapter V

CONCERNING TONGUING

Formerly, the two syllables *tu, ru,** were used to express the attacks of the tongue. But the present virtuosos, who do not teach by *tu, ru,* regard these as being absurd and only serve to hinder the student.**

The attack of the tongue is nothing more than small attacks which the tongue gives behind the opening of the lips, and the small attack is given length or brevity according to the note values. That is to say, if the note is long on which the attack was given, one leaves the note without moving the tongue.

The tongue attacks made on the flute are like the bow strokes made on the violin:

A slur ⌒ under or over two notes, means to play them in the same attack of the tongue

Examples

One also finds three notes slurred, *A*, and four notes slurred, *B* in concertos and sonatas.

One makes several tongue attacks without taking another breath, and one ordinarily does not take a breath until the end of a phrase, *C, D*. See the first book of solos by Mr. Blavet.***

A large slur, *E*, above or under several notes with dots over the notes mean that all notes are to be articulated in the same breath. The dots ... and the small lines ''' over the notes mean the same thing.****

One finds many such passages in the solos and duos for the flute by Locatelli.*****

---

* See Hotteterre, *opere citato*, p. 17.

** Corrette does not continue to give the new syllables to which he alludes, but it is probably that he intends *tootle*, which appears to be the next suggested in flute articulation after *tu, ru*. Confer pp. 6-7.

*** Michel Blavet, *Premier œuvre contenant six sonata pour deux flûtes transversières sans basse* (Paris: 1728). There is no modern edition of this.

**** Confer pp. 6-11 for comparative information regarding articulation.

***** See Pietro Locatelli, *Dodici Sonate a flauto traversiere solo e basso*, Opus II (Amsterdam: 1732); and *Sei Sonate a tre o due violini, o due flauti traversieri e basso*, Opus V (Amsterdam: 1736).

Chapter VI

Article I

OF THE SHAKES OR TRILLS*

The trill is the agitation of two notes struck alternately and as fast as possible.

These are marked in concertos and sonatas by a *t* and in older French music by a + over long notes such as whole, half, or dotted quarters. One begins by beating the trill gently, and in proportion the fingers increase the speed while the air is held steady.**

As a trill is an alternating movement of two notes, it is necessary to borrow to be able to beat it, and this secondary note is never marked in the music.

The borrowed note is always the note just above the one indicated; for example, to make a trill on la, begin it on si, and give an attack of the tongue on si, lowering the finger several times swiftly on the second hole without varying the force of air and without taking a new breath.

It must be noted that the finger which prepares the trill is raised over the hole before blowing.

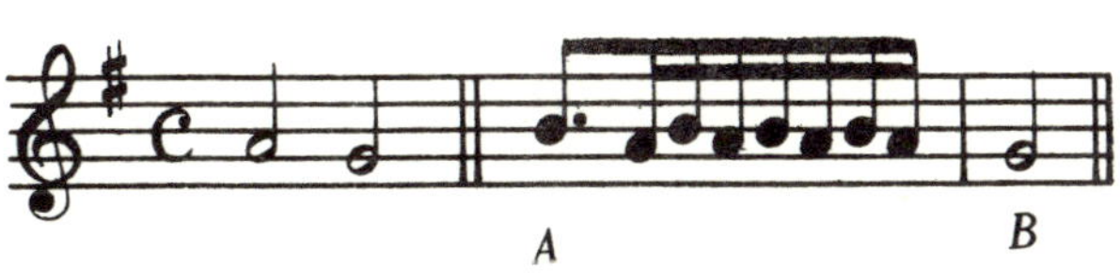

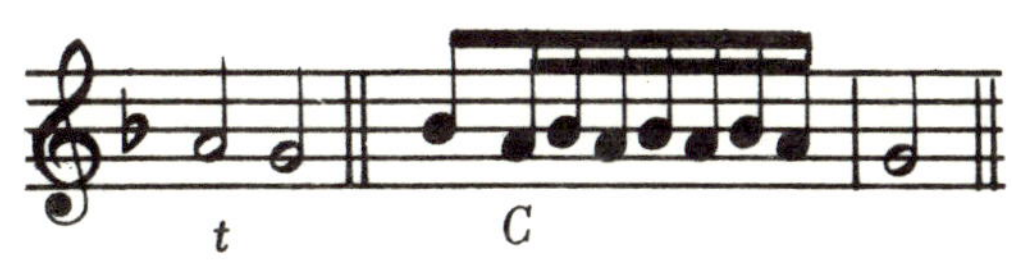

Thus, one always begins the trill on the note above, *A*, and one will finish it by that which is noted *B*, which is the same note *C*, on which is marked a *t*, the sign of the trill most used at the present in music.

Article II

The trill is prepared by a step, or a half step above the note, according to the mode of the piece.

In major mode, as major third in sol, the trill will be made on the second note of the key, la, which will always be hit with si♮. *A*, which is the major third of sol:

---

* *Cadences et tremblemens.* See also Hotteterre, *opere citato*, p. 7; and *Compleat Tutor, opere citato*, p. 241.

** According to Quantz, *opere citato*, p. 102, the shake (or trill) is most effective when played evenly and at uniform speed. Meline, *opere citato*, p. 31, advocates increasing speed and sound during the trill.

The major third is composed of two tones, *F*, *G*. In minor mode, as in sol minor, the trill which is on the second note of the key, la, will always be hit with si ♭, *E*, and that si ♭ is the minor third from sol.

The minor third is composed of a tone and semitone, *H*, *I*.

It is very necessary to know whether one is playing in major or minor mode in order to prepare for the trill on the second note of the key. See Chapter XII.*

Article III

The value of the note over which the sign of the shake is, rules the duration of the trill. The trill will be very long over a whole note 𝅝, and a half note 𝅗𝅥, and shorter over an eighth note 𝅘𝅥𝅮 and quarter note 𝅘𝅥; with a little practice one learns this easily. See the four following tables which demonstrate the manner of preparing the trills of all tones and semitones, according to the manner of the great masters.

Chapter VII

OF THE TURN**

The turn is made like the ordinary shake except that it is followed by two small notes which one can slur or articulate. It is most often made on a long note when going up by conjunct degrees.

Example

NOTE

All the small notes, *A*, *B*, *C* are not counted for any value in the measures; they serve to mark the ornaments. See Chapters X, XI, pp. 34 and 35.***

---

* See p. 55.

** *Double cadence.*

*** See pp. 46-47.

FIRST TABLE OF TRILLS ON DIATONIC TONES

The quarter note marks the note which must be borrowed to prepare the trills. The notes like show the holes on which the fingers beat the trills. The beginning of the arch or on two means that that hole starts the trill, and the end of it shows the hole on which it finishes.

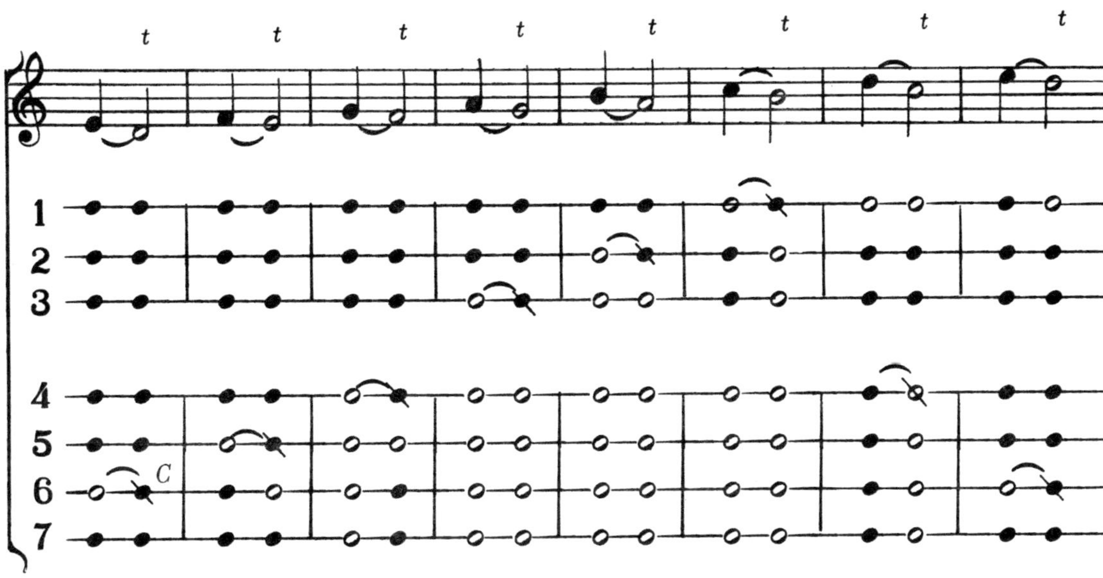

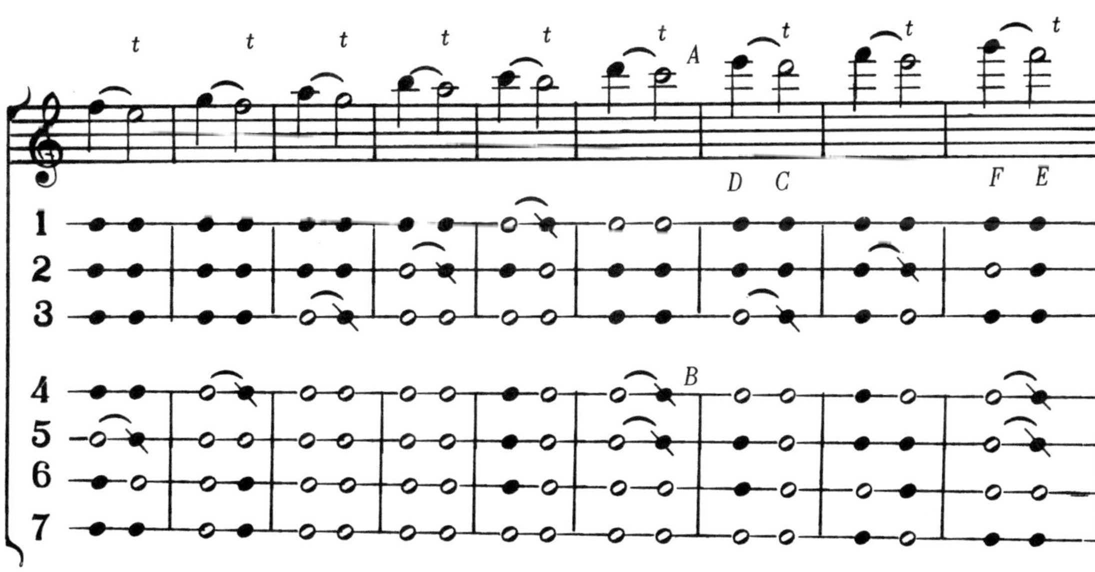

NOTE

The trill on high ut, *A*, is beat with the fourth and fifth fingers, *B*. The trill on ré, *C*, is prepared by mi, *D*. And the trill on fa prepared by sol, *E*, has never been shown.*

---

* It is shown by Hotteterre, *opere citato*, p. 2. Compare these with Quantz, *opere citato*, p. 105.

SECOND TABLE OF TRILLS ON DIATONIC TONES PREPARED BY A SHARP ♯ OR A FLAT ♭

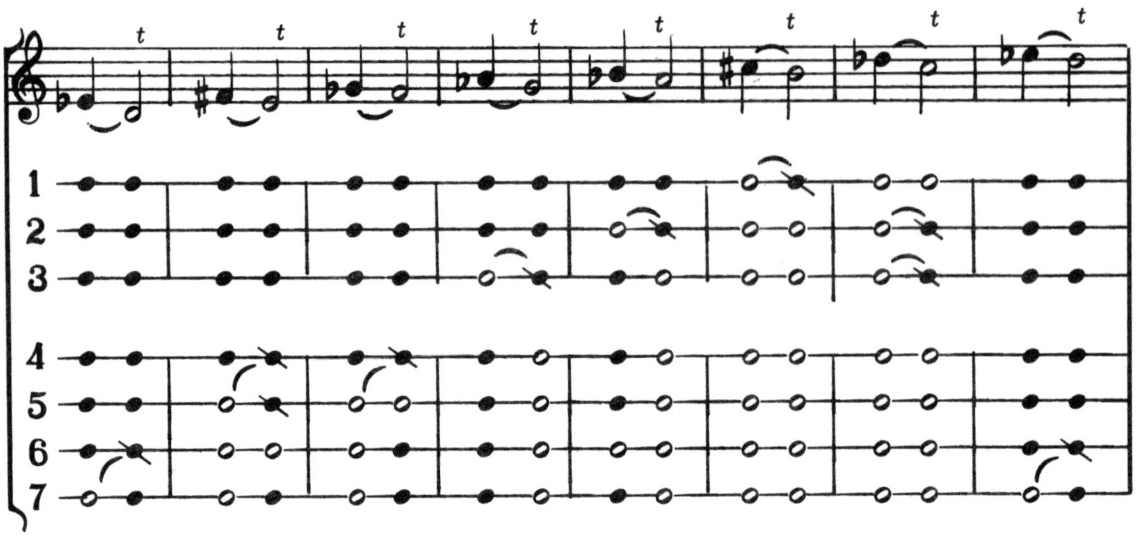

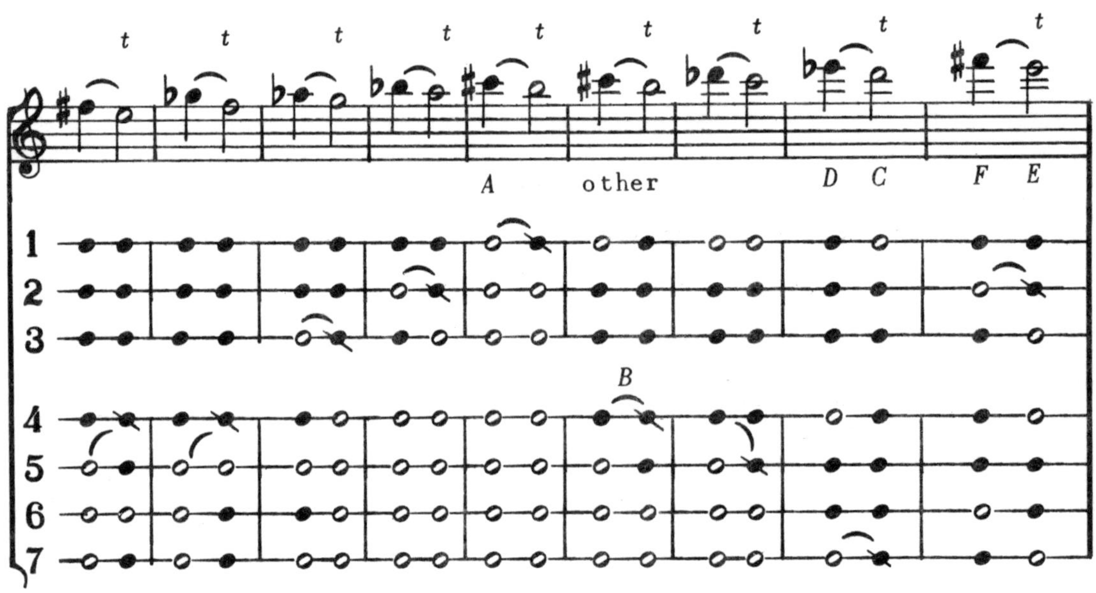

NOTE

The first way to make the trill of high si prepared by ut♯, *A*, is good for fast pieces like allegros and prestos of sonatas. The other way of fingering the same trill is very good in adagios or in tender pieces. In this way, it is more brilliant, but the other is easier in virtuoso pieces. The trill of high ré, *C*, prepared by mi♭, *D*, is very rare. The trill of mi♮, *E*, prepared by fa♯, *F*, has never been shown.*

---

* Corrette is the first to show this trill.

THIRD TABLE OF TRILLS ON THE SHARPS ♯ AND FLATS ♭ PREPARED BY A NATURAL NOTE

The trill on high mi♭, *A*, prepared by fa, *B*, can only be made by covering half of the fifth hole. The trill on fa♯ prepared by sol♮. *E*, has never been shown.*

---

* Corrette is the first to show this trill.

FOURTH TABLE. TRILLS ON SHARPS ♯ PREPARED BY SHARPS

(See fifth Table)

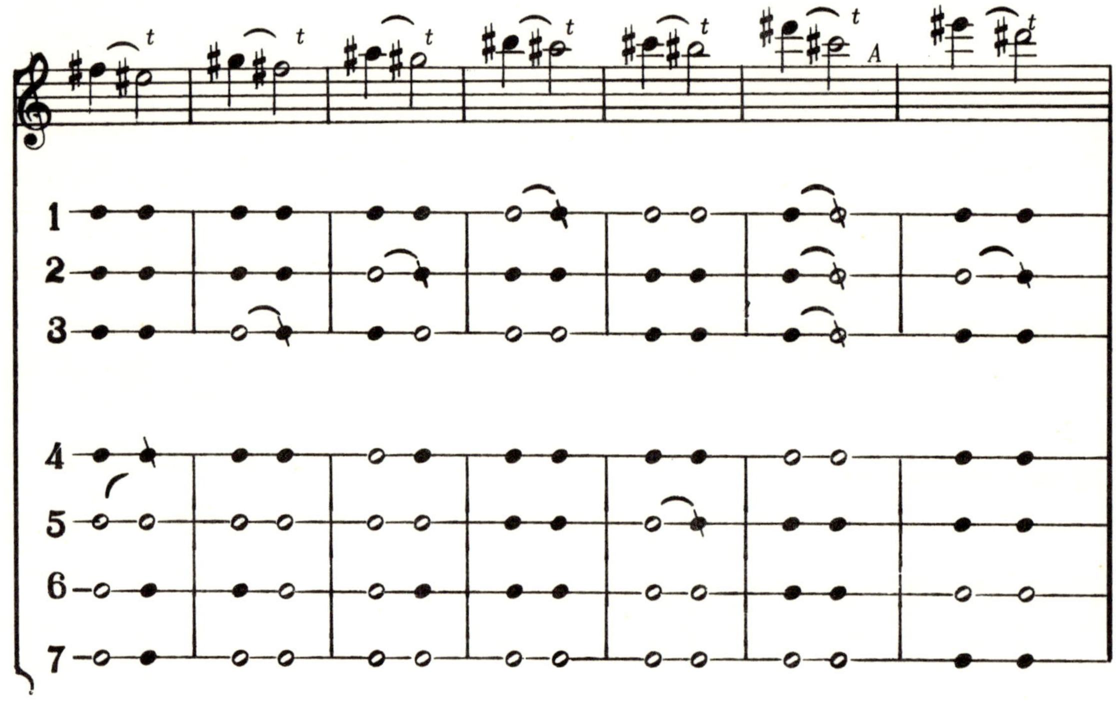

The trill on ut# prepared by ré♯, *A*, has never been shown, but it can be made on all flutes regardless of the way they are pierced.*

---

* Corrette is the first to show this trill, which is very weak.

FIFTH TABLE OF THE ACCOUNT OF TRILLS ON SHARPS ♯ WITH THESE AND ON FLATS ♭ WHICH CAN BE QUICKLY MADE AND WHICH THE FINGERS PREPARE AT THE SAME HOLES

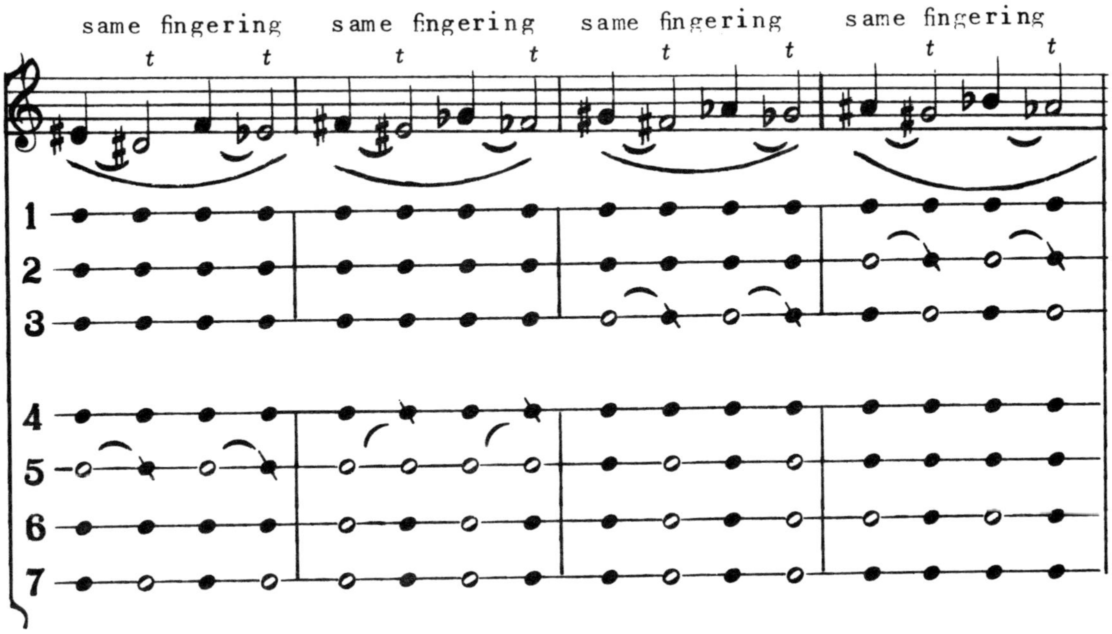

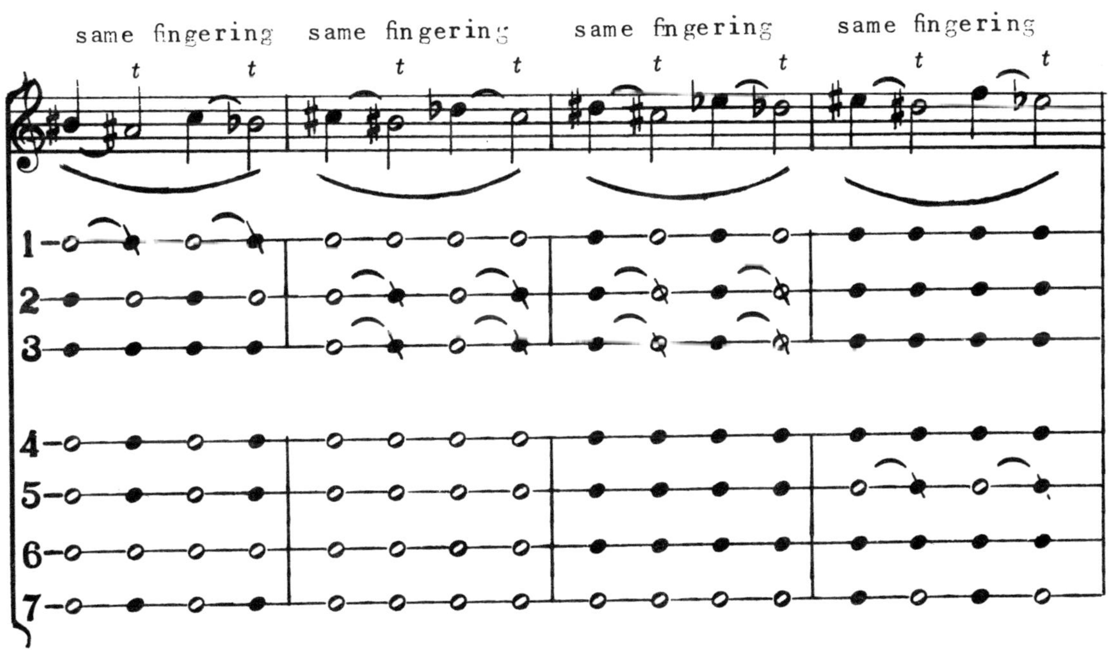

The trill on ré♯ prepared by mi♯ is the same as the trill on mi♭ prepared by fa♮, as ré♯ is fingered like mi♭ and mi♯ like fa♮. Thus, the other trills are notated and shown by the above table. This is relative to the explanation of the sharps and flats of which we had given an account in Chapter IV, p. 16.*

---

* See pp. 27 ff.

CONTINUATION OF THE FIFTH TABLE OF THE ACCOUNT OF TRILLS ON SHARPS AND FLATS

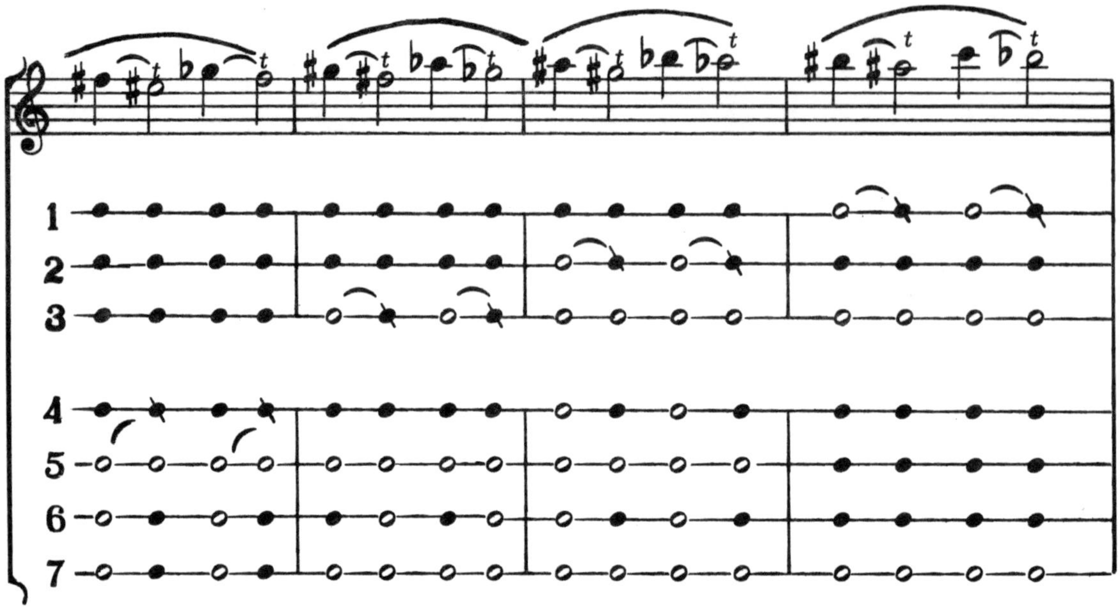

Chapter VIII

TO EXPLAIN THE MANNER OF MAKING THE SOFTENING* ON THE TONES AND SEMITONES

The softening is made with a finger which is well extended over the hole and below the last hole which is covered. One must observe that the finger does not cover the hole on which the softening is made, but it is lowered softly and held in the air in finishing except on the second ré.

The softening is done to swell and diminish the tone. This ornament is extremely moving in tender pieces on long notes. It is indicated by the sign  but is rarely ⟪marked⟫.

Table

Concerning the fingers which are employed to make the softening for each tone and semitone:

For low ré♮, *A*, all the holes are covered, and one shakes the flute with the right hand.

In the same way, one makes the softening on low ré♯ or mi♭, *B*.

For mi♮, *C*, the softening is made at the edge of the sixth hole.

For fa♮, *D*, and fa♯, *E*, at the fifth hole.

For sol♮, *F*, it is made in two ways. Observe: at the edge of the fourth hole or full upon the fifth hole. This last way is the easier.

For sol♯, or la♭, *G*, at the edge of the third hole or by shaking the flute.

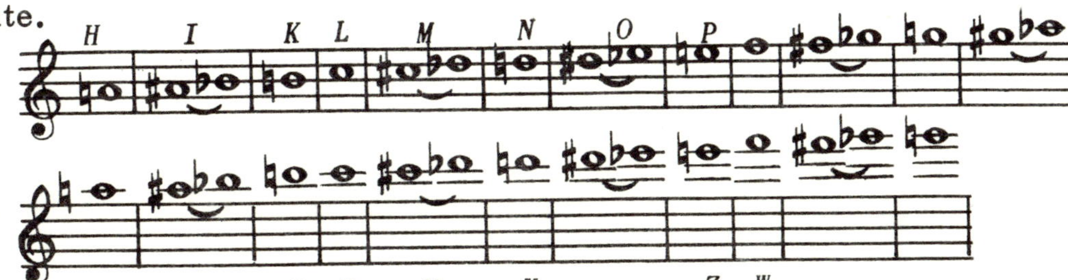

For la♮, *H*, at the edge of the fourth hole. One can make it at the third hole, but it is not so easy.

For la♯ or si♭, *I*, at the sixth hole full.

For si♮, *K*, full upon the fourth hole.**

For ut♮, *L*, full upon the fourth hole.

---

* *Flatemens*. For the effect of this ornament, confer p. 12. For comparison, see Loulié, *opere citato*, p. 77, who illustrates it thus: 

** Hotteterre, *opere citato*, p. 23, advocates making the softening upon the third hole.

For ut♯, or ré♭, *M*, full upon the third hole. Former players * made it at the second hole, but it is worth nothing and lowers the tone by a comma. See p. 17.**

For ré♮, *N*, full upon the second hole. One must begin and finish by covering the hole.

For ré♯ or mi♭, *O*, upon the first hole. One must cover it before and after the softening. One can also make it in shaking the flute with the right hand, as we have said of low ré♯ or mi♭.

From mi♮, *P*, to la♮, *Q*, the softening is made like those of the octave below. See *C, D, E, F, G,* and *H*.

For la♯ or si♭, *R*, at the edge of the fourth hole.

For si♮, *S*, full upon the fourth hole, as with the octave below, *K*.

For ut♯ or ré♭, *V*, full upon the sixth hole.

For ré♮, *X*, the finger at the edge of the fourth hole.***

For ré♯ or mi♭, *Z*, the finger at the edge of the third hole.

For the other high tones, the softening can only be made by shaking the flute with the right hand, *W*.

Chapter IX

TO EXPLAIN THE MANNER OF MAKING THE MORDENT ****

The mordent is made by beating a finger one or several times on the nearest hole to the tone or semitone where one wants to realize it.

The simple mordent is made by beating the finger full upon the hole. One moves by one hole the finger that is trained to cover the hole.

The double mordent is made by beating the finger several times upon a hole, and generally this mordent is always made on an open hole.

Table

Concerning the fingers which are employed to make the mordent for each tone and semitone:

---

* Here, Corrette obviously refers to Hotteterre who said to make it at the second hole. See Hotteterre, *loco citato*.

** See p. 31.

*** See Hotteterre, *loco citato*, who says to make it "on the second hole, as its octave."

**** *Battement*. In the eighteenth century, the French *battement* was also known as the beat in English. Hotteterre, *opere citato*, pp. 9-10, uses the sign / to indicate the beat. Quantz, *opere citato*, p. 98, makes the distinction between the *pincé* and the *battement*, that the *battement* does not have the opening appoggiatura.

For low ré, *A*, ré♯ or mi♭, one does not make the mordent. As the mordent is made from the note below, it would be ridiculous to try it on low ré because this is the lowest note on the flute.

For mi♮, *C*, it is made on the sixth hole.

For fa♮, *D*, and fa♯, *E*, on the fifth hole.

For sol♮, *F*, on the fourth hole.

For sol♯ or la♭, *G*, and la♮, *H*, on the third hole.

For la♯ or si♭, *I*, and si♮, *K*, on the second hole.

For ut♮, *L*, on the fourth and fifth holes, two fingers beating at the same time.

For ut♯ or ré♭, *M*, on the first hole.

Continuation of the Table of Mordents

For ré♮, *N*, on the fourth hole when the key of the piece does not demand ut♯, but if one plays ré, it is necessary to make the mordent with ut♯, which is the leading tone of ré. Then one will make it on the second and third holes, beating two fingers at the same time. It is also necessary that one be careful to cover the holes well in beginning and ending the mordent.

It will always be made with ut♯ if the sharp is in the key, as in si with a major third, in fa♯, etc. See Chapter XII.*

For ré♯ or mi♭, *O*, one can only draw a false tone.

From mi♮, *P*, up to si♮, *Q*, the mordents are made like those of the lower octave. See those over *C, D, E, F, G, H, I, K*.

For ut♮, *R*, on the first hole or on the sixth.

For ut♯ or ré♭, *S*, on the fifth hole.

For ré♮, *T*, on the fourth hole, and for ré♯ or mi♭, *V*, one can make it on the fourth hole by making it very short.

For mi♮, *X*, on the third hole.

For fa♮ and fa♯, *Y*, of the third octave, one cannot make mordents.

For sol♮, *Z*, on the fourth hole and the key closed.

---

* See p. 55.

Chapter X

OF THE APPOGGIATURA * AND THE SPRINGER **

The appoggiatura is marked by the small note, ♪.

The appoggiatura is frequently made when one ascends by conjunct degrees of an eighth note and a quarter note, *A*.

Appoggiatura

The small line ⌒ over or under the small note ♪ and the large one ♩, means that they must be made in the same attack of the tongue.

The springer is a small note which one borrows on the end of the value of a note on which one wants to make it. *C*, is made in the same attack of the tongue as the note preceding it, *D*.

When this ornament is not marked, one can make it on long notes when they descend by conjunct degrees, *E*, *F*.

One can also make it when there are several notes of the same degree, *G*, *H*.

Chapter XI

OF THE TREMOLO ***

In order to make the *martellement*, one must beat it on the lower note, *A*, hereafter continuing to beat on the holes with two or three quick attacks from above, making it different from the trill, which is beaten downward, *B*.

---

* *Port de voix*. Corrette's demonstration of this is the same as that of Loulié, *opere citato*, p. 73, and Hotteterre, *opere citato*, pp. 20-21.

** *Accent*. See John Playford, *An Introduction to the Skill of Musick* (London: 1655), Table of Graces; and Thomas Mace, *Musick's Monument* (London: T. Radcliffe and N. Thomson, 1676), p. 108.

*** *Martellement*. Corrette's description of this ornament corresponds with that of Hotteterre, *opere citato*, p. 9 and Rousseau, *opere citato*, p. 220.

A *B*

The *martellement* is composed of a double appoggiatura and a double mordent.

One can make it on the final note when it is preceded by an appoggiatura, *A*.

Another Martellement

In the Italian Manner

In adagios, the Italians sometimes make the appoggiatura, *C*, as long as the note that follows it, or longer, *D*, and then make the *martellement*.

But to make it well, one must soften the sound of the flute.

After having learned all the ornaments one will find practiced on all occasions, one will find this to be most appropriate, for it must be pointed out that ornaments are not always marked in the music. This is why it is good and even necessary in the beginning to play pieces where the ornaments are marked. See the pieces and preludes which are in this book.

Moreover, it is necessary to remember that in order to execute the ornaments and virtuoso passages well, one must never rush them, however fast they can be played. Rather take one's time, prepare one's fingers, and execute with easiness and liberty, without forcing the wind, and without rushing the meter.

Vaudeville

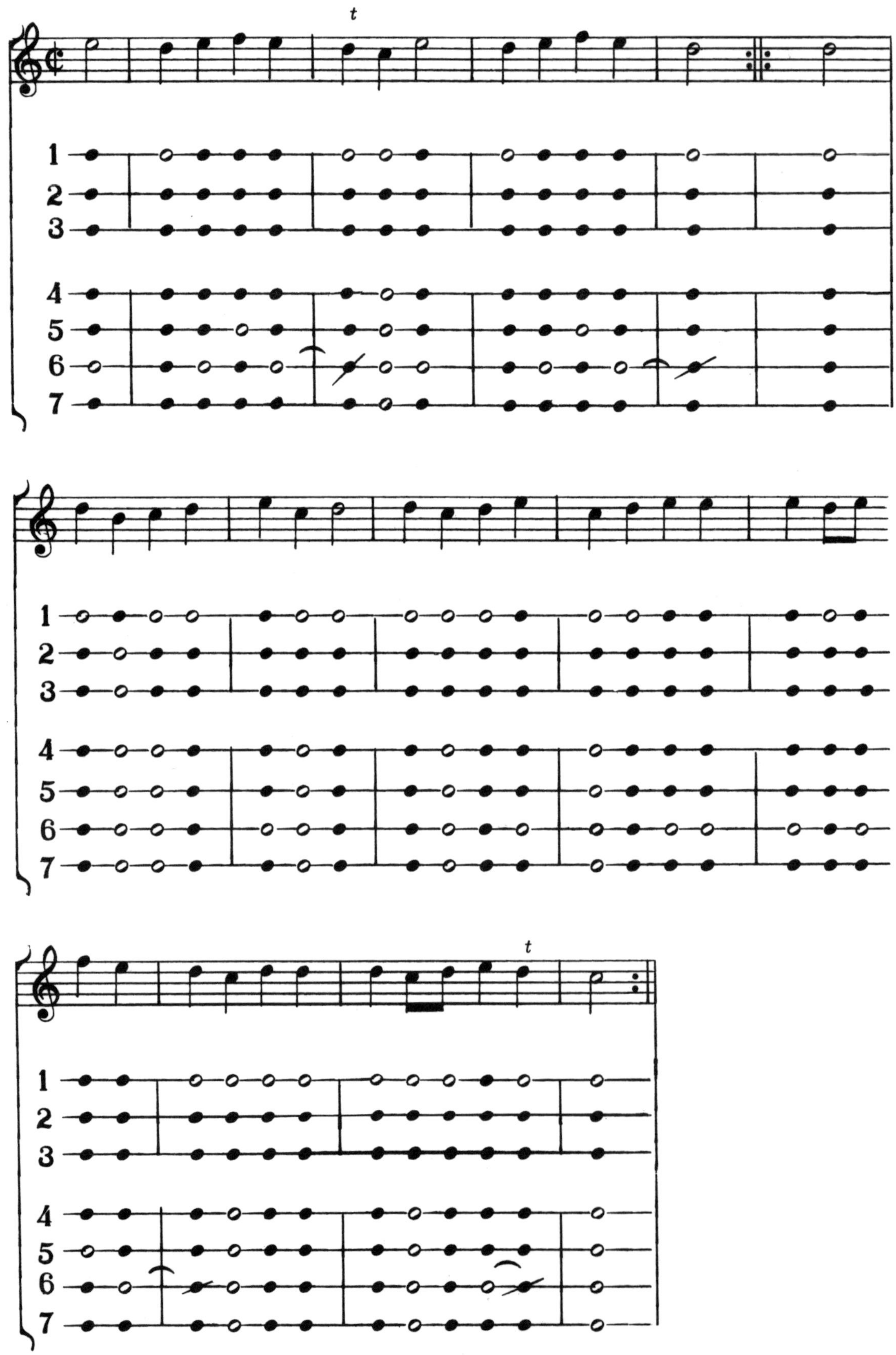

Vaudeville

The ♯ by the clef affects all notes found on the same line.

Minuet by Händel

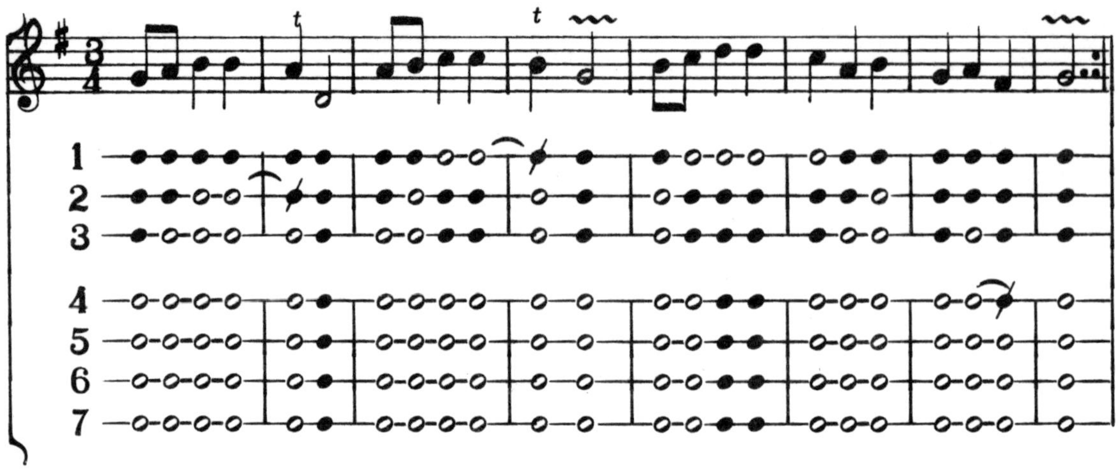

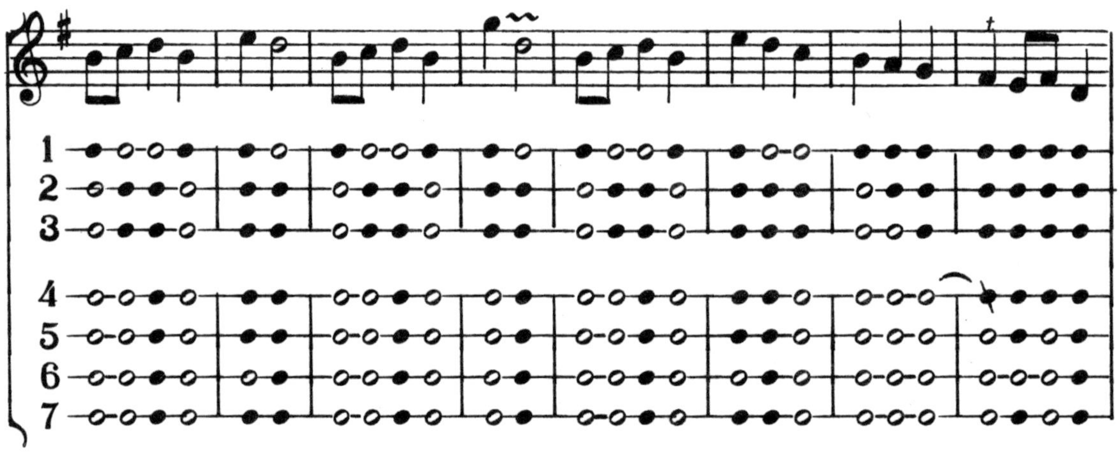

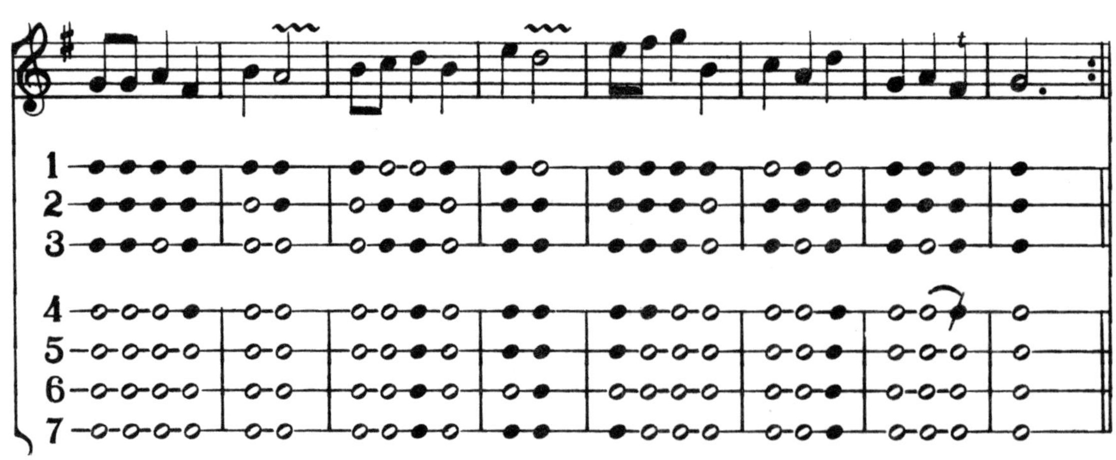

Wake Up, Sleeping Beauty

Italian Minuet

Rondeau

Allemande in Sonata VIII

Rondeau

Gavotte from Dardanus

Gavotte in Sonata IX

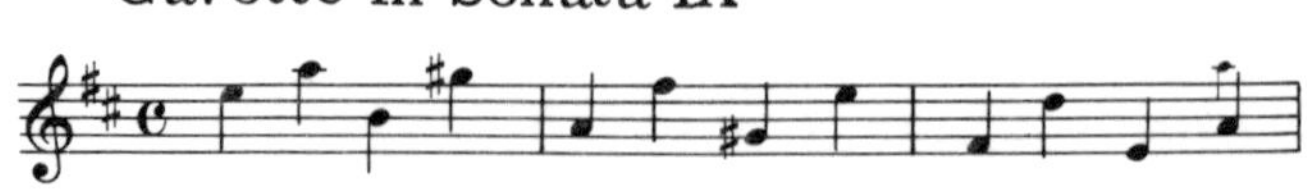

* Confer p. 14.

Sarabande

Fanfare

Fanfare by Dandrieu*

---

* See Jean-F. Dandrieu, "Première Fanfare," in the *Livre de Pieces de Clavecin... les Charactères de la Guerre* (Paris: Boivin, 1724), p. 11. The fanfare, as found in Dandrieu's work, is in C major. Corrette has transposed it to D.

Minuet from Dardanus*

Brunette

---

* Rameau, *opere citato*, p. 268. Confer pp. 14-15.

Chapter XII

IN ORDER TO LEARN IF A PIECE IS IN MAJOR OR MINOR MODE

The treatment of a song is always composed in either major or minor mode. The difference of the mode is perceived by the third or mediant note of the key. This third is named major third in major mode as in ut, *A*, and minor third in minor mode as in ut♭, *B*. *

Moreover, it must be pointed out that it is from the final note that one knows the key of the piece, considering that the piece can begin on the dominant or on the mediant, either of which makes perfect harmony with the bass.

For the third to be major, it is necessary that one finds three semitones in its interval, *C*. If one finds but two, it is a sign that the third is minor, *E*.

TABLE OF THE MAJOR AND MINOR MODES

The 12 Major Modes

The 12 Minor Modes

---

* Corrette obviously means the key of c minor.

Chapter XIII

OF THE ART OF IMPROVISATION

The prelude* is a kind of caprice which is ordinarily composed on the spot before playing a piece. One can express it in the same meter as the beginning of the piece. In order to improvise well, it is necessary to observe if the mode of the music one is going to play is major or minor, and improvise in the same key. When one plays alone without accompaniment, one can compose a longer prelude.

One can then modulate in the way that one wishes, to make the passages fast or slow by conjunct or disjunct degrees, according to what is present in the imagination.

The following sixteen preludes ** can serve as models.

As a song cannot be varied enough, above all it should never all be in the same key, *** but it is permissable to pass into another key.**** That passage is made by means of the leading tone, and the leading tone is always a semitone below the key note in a major or minor key.

Example

To improvise well and at the same time execute well all kinds of music, it is necessary to know the names of the intervals which occur sometimes in groups, ***** one always counts from the lowest note.

In scores, particularly of motets, cantatas, and operas, one sometimes finds the first and second parts on the same staff; thus, the first part plays the higher notes, and the second the lower ones. The four preludes in duo here can serve as examples.

---

* Brossard, *opere citato*, p. 183, "prelude is a flourish or an irregular air, which a musician plays off-hand, to try if his instrument be in tune, and so lead him into the piece to be played." According to Quantz, *opere citato*, p. 179, the French did not perform this embellishment.

** Corrette illustrates twenty-nine preludes, but only sixteen introduce new intervals.

*** *Ton.* **** *Mode.*

***** *Batteries* are taken in this context to mean common intervals which occur repeatedly in a passage.

Names of Intervals which can be Transposed into All Keys

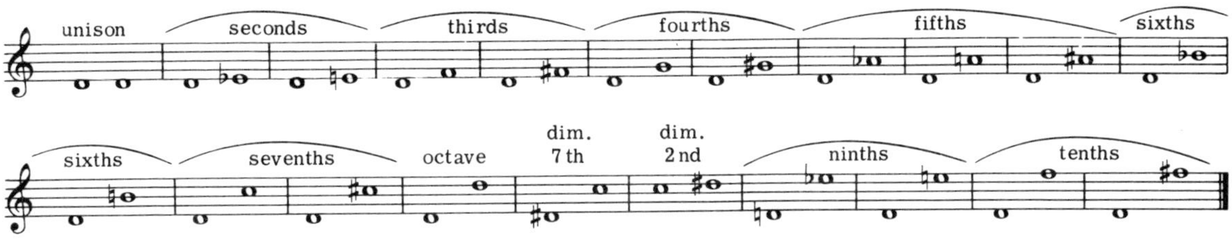

Model for improvising

8. Prelude

9. Prelude

10. Prelude

11. Prelude by fifths

12. Prelude

13. Prelude by sixths

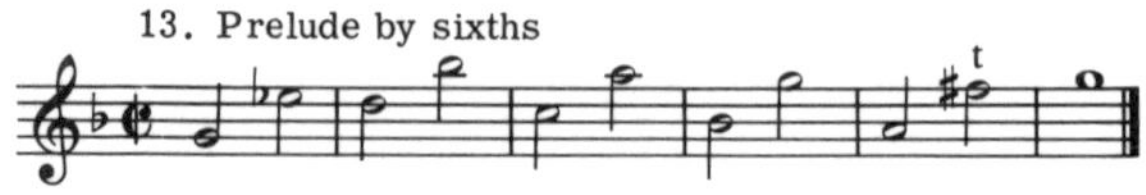

14. Prelude by groups of sixths

15. Prelude by sevenths

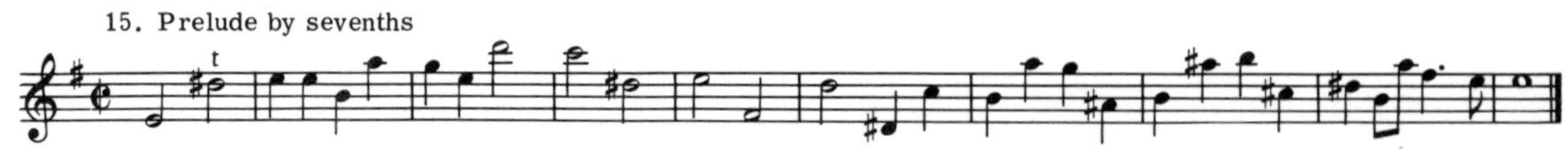

16. Prelude by octaves

17. Prelude

18. Prelude

19. Prelude

20. Prelude

21. Prelude

22. Prelude

23. Prelude

24. Prelude

25. Prelude

26. Duo Prelude

27. Prelude

28. Duo Prelude

29. Duo Prelude

Chapter XIV

ON THE MANNER OF TRANSPOSITION

To transpose one might say is to play in a key or mode different from that which is given. For example, if a piece is in ut and one wishes to transpose it to a key one tone higher which would be ré, it is necessary to imagine playing in the C-clef placed on the third line. If one wishes to execute the same piece in ut one tone lower which would be si♭, one must imagine playing in the C-clef placed on the fourth line. Thus, it is necessary to know the notes in the two C-clefs, *A, B.*

Example

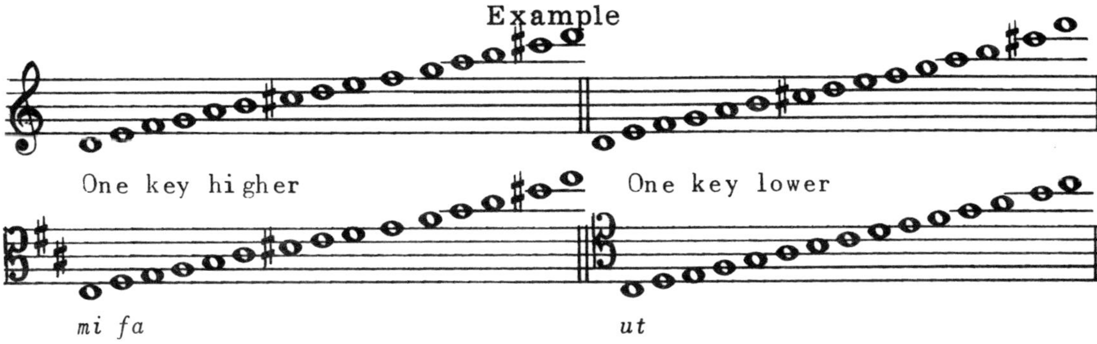

On the transverse flute, one can play a quartertone, a semitone, and three-quarters of a tone higher or lower, without transposing the name of the notes by means of replacing parts, as we have said in Chapter I, p. 7, *

These three or four higher or lower, hardly ever occur in concert for there are more correct transpositions in the range of the flute. It is easy to see that the transposition is only to accomodate the range or extent of the voice or ((other)) instruments.

NOTE

When one transposes a step higher in a minor key or mode, one must substitute a ♯ in the key signature on the sixth note of the key, *C.*

---

* See p. 24.

Chapter XV

OF THE SIMILARITY IN FIGURES THAT CAN BE MADE ON THE TRANSVERSE FLUTE AND THE MANNER OF PLAYING LOWER NOTES OF THE VIOLIN SONATAS ON THAT INSTRUMENT

Even though one cannot make the notes on the transverse flute, nevertheless, one can express them by playing the harmony notes one after another, *A*.

Example

Range of the fourth string on the violin

This is very useful when one wishes to play violin sonatas and concertos where the arpeggio is found very often.

Then one can form an arpeggio according to the example above when the notes do not descend or go lower than ré in the G-clef, which is the last note on the transverse flute. The notes below the range of the flute, *B,* can be transposed to the octave above, *C, D*.

Other examples are drawn from the works (Opus 5) of Corelli, Édition d'Hol. or Angleterre.*

The smaller notes mark the notes that the flute plays an octave higher than those which are for the fourth string on the violin.

Low ut♯ *E,* is made by covering all the holes as for low ré, only turning the mouthpiece of the flute inwards.

---

* See Archangelo Corelli, *Twelve Sonata Solos for Violin and Bass,* Opus V (London: J. Walsh, circa 1710).

EXTRACT OF THE GENERAL PRIVILEGE

By the grace and consent of the King given at Versailles, the twenty-first day of January, 1735, signed Sainson, Mr. _______, music master, is granted permission to print all kinds of music, both vocal and instrumental of his own composition. During the time and space of six consecutive years, it is expressly forbidden to all people, whatever their quality or condition, to engrave to have engraved, to sell or have sold, or to counterfeit, even to extract anything whatsoever under pretext of corrections and changes in titles or otherwise, under fine of six thousand pounds penalty and the confiscation of said counterfeited copies, insofar as it is marked plainly on the original.

Registered by the ninth registrar of the Royal Chamber of the Paris Bookstore, N. 54, Folio 46, according to the rule of 1723, Paris, 17th of February 1735.

Signed

G. Martin Syndie

The examples have been furnished.

UNSERE VERÖFFENTLICHUNGEN
OUR PUBLICATIONS

VERÖFFENTLICHUNGEN MITTELALTERLICHER MUSIKHANDSCHRIFTEN

PUBLICATIONS OF MEDIÆVAL MUSICAL MANUSCRIPTS

Vol. I	Madrid 20486	DM 32
Vol. II	Wolfenbüttel 1099 Helmst. (1206)	DM 200
Vol. III	Eine zentrale Quelle der Notre Dame-Musik. A Central Source of Notre-Dame Polyphony	DM 60
Vol. IV	Paris, *nouv. acq. frç. 13531 & lat. 11411*	DM 30
Vol. V	Worcester, *Add. 68,* Westminster *33327* & Madrid *192*	DM 36
Vol. VI	Oxford, lat. litur. d 20 & Chicago 654 App.	DM 48
Vol. VII	Opera omnia Faugues	DM 60
Vol. VIII	Sevilla, 5-I-43 & Paris, nouv. acq. frç. 4379	DM 72
Vol. IX	Carmina Burana	DM 250
Vol. X	Firenze, Pluteo 29,1 (Pars I)	DM 160
Vol. XI	Firenze, Pluteo 29,1 (Pars II)	DM 160

MUSICAL THEORISTS IN TRANSLATION

Vol. I	Anonymus IV	DM 30
Vol. II	Robert de Handlo	DM 28
Vol. III	Nivers, *Treatise on the Composition of Music*	DM 20
Vol. IV	Huygens, *Use and Nonuse of the Organ in the Churches of the United Netherlands*	DM 20
Vol. V	Bernier, *Principles of Composition*	DM 24
Vol. VI	Loulié, *Elements or Principles of Music*	DM 50
Vol. VII	Bacilly, *A Commentary upon the Art of Proper Singing*	DM 100

GESAMTAUSGABEN - COLLECTED WORKS

Vol. I	Faugues *(Gesamtausgabe, Collected Works)*	DM 60
Vol. II/1	A. Rener, *Collected Works.* I: The Motets	DM 48
Vol. III/1	Goudimel, *Collected Works.* I: Psalm Motets Vol. I	DM 60
Vol. III/2	Goudimel, *Collected Works.* 2: Psalm Motets Vol. 2	DM 60
Vol. III/9	Goudimel, *Collected Works.* 9: 150 Psalms of 1564/1565 („Jaqui)	DM 60
Vol. III/10	Goudimel, *Collected Works.* 10: 150 Psalms of 1568/1580 („St. André")	DM 120
Vol. IV/1	Cabezón, *Collected Works.* 1: Duos, Kyries, Variations etc.	DM 64

WISSENSCHAFTLICHE ABHANDLUNGEN - MUSICOLOGICAL STUDIES

Vol. I	L. Dittmer, *Auszug aus The Worcester Music Fragments*	DM 4
Vol. II	G. Schuetze, *An Introduction to Faugues*	DM 42
Vol. III	E. Trumble, *Fauxbourdon, an Historical Survey,* I	DM 30
Vol. IV	L. Spiess, *Historical Musicology*	DM 32
Vol. V	S. Levarie, *Fundamentals of Harmony*	DM 7,80
Vol. VI	E. Southern, *The Buxheim Organ Book*	DM 60
Vol. VII	L. Dittmer, *Friedrich Ludwig, Repertorium organorum* ... I, 1	vergriffen
Vol. VIII	C. Jacobs, *Tempo Notation in Renaissance Spain*	DM 40
Vol. IX	E. Thomson, *An Introduction to Philippe (?) Caron*	DM 12
Vol. X	H. Tischler, *A Structural Analysis of Mozart's Piano Concertos*	DM 72
Vol. XI	V. Mattfeld, *Georg Rhaw's Publications for Vespers*	DM 60
Vol. XII	E. Borroff, *An Introduction to Elisabeth-Claude Jacquet de la Guerre*	DM 48
Vol. XIII	F. J. Smith, *The Speculum Musicæ of Jacobus Leodiensis I*	DM 24
Vol. XIV	J. Travis, *Miscellanea musica celtica*	DM 40
Vol. XV	C. W. Brockett, *Antiphons, Reponsories, and Other Chants of the Mozarabic Rite*	DM 120
Vol. XVI	F. Crane, *Materials for the Study of the Fifteenth-Century Basse Danse*	DM 60
Vol. XVII	L. Dittmer, *Friedrich Ludwig, Repertorium organorum* ... II	DM 80

MIKROFILME - MICROFILMS

I Studies of Music in the Middle Ages	DM 72
II U. Chevallier, *Repertorium hymnologicum* I-VI	DM 48

Die Preise verstehen sich in DM; andere sind Richtpreise. Official prices are in German Marks.

THE INSTITUTE OF MEDIÆVAL MUSIC, LTD.

1653 West 8th Street, Brooklyn, New York 11223, U.S.A.